Italian Food Air Fryer Cookbook for UK

Simple and Crispy Italian Food Air Fryer Recipes Bring You Authentic Italian Flavour and Make Every Meal Effortless and Delicious

Patrice Blandford

© **Copyright 2024 – All Rights Reserved.**

The content contained within this book may not be reproduced, duplicated or transmitted without direct written permission from the author or the publisher.

Under no circumstances will any blame or legal responsibility be held against the publisher, or author, for any damages, reparation, or monetary loss due to the information contained within this book, either directly or indirectly.

Legal Notice:

This book is copyright protected. It is only for personal use. You cannot amend, distribute, sell, use, quote or paraphrase any part, or the content within this book, without the consent of the author or publisher.

Disclaimer Notice:

Please note the information contained within this document is for educational and entertainment purposes only. All effort has been executed to present accurate, up to date, reliable, complete information. No warranties of any kind are declared or implied. Readers acknowledge that the author is not engaged in the rendering of legal, financial, medical or professional advice. The content within this book has been derived from various sources. Please consult a licensed professional before attempting any techniques outlined in this book.

By reading this document, the reader agrees that under no circumstances is the author responsible for any losses, direct or indirect, that are incurred as a result of the use of the information contained within this document, including, but not limited to, errors, omissions, or inaccuracies.

Table of Contents

01	**Introduction**	17	Parmesan Roasted Cauliflower
		18	Roasted Courgette and Squash
02	**Fundamentals of an Air Fryer**	18	Roasted Ratatouille
		19	Stuffed Bell Peppers
		19	Homemade Pita Pizza
08	**Chapter 1 Breakfast Recipes**	20	Quick Fingerling Potatoes
08	Breakfast Bacon Egg Cups	20	Pesto Gnocchi
08	Ham and Egg Bake	20	Herbed Mushrooms with White Wine
09	Tomato and Egg Bake	21	Mixed Veggies Pancakes
09	Spinach and Egg Ramekins	21	Roasted Root Vegetable Medley
09	Prosciutto Egg Cups	22	Stuffed Tomatoes
10	Smoked Trout Frittata	22	Healthy Courgette Fritters
10	Sausage and Tomato Frittata	23	Cherry Tomato Pasta
11	Spinach Frittata with Tomato and Onion	23	Tomato Pizza with Courgette
11	Oatmeal Raisin Muffins		
12	Soft Date Bread	**24**	**Chapter 3 Snack & Appetizer Recipes**
12	Classic Cinnamon Toast	24	Strawberry Bruschetta
13	Ham and Cheese Breakfast Casserole	24	Tasty Arancini
13	Kale and Cheese Omelet	25	Pizza Toast
13	Egg in Avocado	25	Cheesy Broccoli Bites
14	Bell Pepper and Summer Squash Frittata	25	Italian Parmesan Tomato Crisps
14	Cranberry Harvest Granola	26	Crispy Fried Ravioli
		26	Mini Portobello Mushroom Pizza
15	**Chapter 2 Vegetable and Side Recipes**	27	Pesto Stuffed Tomatoes
15	Aubergine Parmesan	27	Spanakopita Rolls
15	Parmesan Asparagus	28	Crispy Mozzarella Sticks
16	Brussels Sprouts with Parmesan Breadcrumbs	28	Mozzarella Cheese Bites
16	Cheesy Spinach Stuffed Pasta Shells	29	Parmesan Aubergines Chips
17	Roasted Spinach with Feta	29	Courgette Pizza Boats
		29	Pasta Chips

30 Chapter 4 Poultry Recipes

- 30 Chicken Milanese with Basil Tomato Sauce
- 30 Easy Pesto Chicken Breasts
- 31 Lemon Chicken Thighs
- 31 Crispy Crumbed Chicken Cutlets
- 32 Herbed Roasted Whole Chicken
- 32 Mustard-Herb Chicken Drumsticks
- 33 Sausage Stuffed Chicken Breast
- 33 Classic Chicken Parmigiana
- 34 Spinach Stuffed Chicken Breasts
- 34 Chicken Spiedini
- 35 Parmesan Chicken Meatballs
- 35 Herbed Roasted Turkey Breast
- 36 Homemade Turkey Burgers
- 36 Turkey Pepperoni Calzones
- 37 Chicken Parmesan Meatballs with Pasta
- 37 Parmesan Chicken Tenders
- 38 Chicken Parmesan
- 38 Chicken Margherita
- 39 Italian Marinated Chicken Thighs
- 39 Italian Stuffed Chicken Breasts
- 40 Classic Chicken Piccata

41 Chapter 5 Red Meat Recipes

- 41 Herbed Beef Roast
- 41 Lemony Garlic Flank Steak
- 42 Crispy Beef Stromboli
- 42 Garlic Steak Bites
- 43 Ground Beef Stuffed Bell Peppers
- 43 Ground Beef Foil Packets with Vegetables
- 44 Pistachio-Crusted Rack of Lamb
- 44 Pesto Rack of Lamb
- 45 Herbed Lamb Chops
- 45 Lemony Garlic Lamb Chops
- 46 Lamb Steak and Pasta
- 46 Herbed Pork Chops
- 47 Rosemary Pork Loin
- 47 Ham and Pepperoni Sliders
- 48 Pork Meatballs
- 48 Stuffed Pork Roll
- 49 Beef Lasagna
- 49 Italian Sausages with Bell Peppers
- 50 Spiced Pork Tenderloin
- 50 Crumb-Crusted Rack of Lamb
- 51 Flank Steak Pinwheels

52 Chapter 6 Fish & Seafood Recipes

- 52 Crispy Tilapia Milanese
- 52 Rosemary Salmon
- 53 Dill Cod with Green Beans
- 53 Lemony Herbed Cod
- 54 Spiced Tilapia with Caper Sauce
- 54 Healthy Salmon with Asparagus
- 55 Clams Oreganata
- 55 Crispy Parmesan Shrimp
- 56 Classic Shrimp Scampi
- 56 Scallops in Butter Sauce
- 57 Dill Salmon Cakes
- 57 Garlic Butter Lobster Tails with Olives
- 58 Roasted Tuna with Linguine
- 58 Roasted Tuna with Capers
- 58 Simple Cod with Pesto
- 59 Tasty Shrimp Risotto
- 59 Lemon Roasted Whole Branzino
- 60 Spicy Roasted Salmon
- 60 Parmesan Crusted Tilapia

61 Chapter 7 Dessert Recipes

- 61 Cheesecake Bites
- 61 Sweet Dough Balls
- 62 Easy Vanilla Biscotti
- 62 Banana Yoghurt Cake
- 63 Semolina Cake
- 63 Perfect Chocolate Cheesecake
- 64 Lemon Ricotta Cheesecake
- 64 Sweet Apple Pie
- 65 Chocolate Croissants
- 65 Peach Cobbler
- 66 Delicious Cannoli
- 66 Honey Cake with Almonds and Pistachios
- 67 Strawberry Cheesecake
- 67 Chocolate Cream Puffs

67 Conclusion

Introduction

Embark on a culinary journey through Italy with the Colourful Italian Food Air Fryer Cookbook for the UK. This vibrant collection is your gateway to authentic Italian flavours reimagined for the modern air fryer. Whether you're a seasoned cook or just starting your culinary adventures, this cookbook brings the charm of Italian cuisine into your kitchen with simplicity and ease.

Inside, you'll discover a delightful array of recipes inspired by traditional Italian cooking, adapted to save time while preserving flavour. From golden, crispy arancini and herb-crusted chicken Milanese to light, airy focaccia and indulgent tiramisu, this cookbook offers something for everyone. The air fryer's efficiency ensures you can create healthier versions of Italian favourites with less oil but all the deliciousness intact.

Designed with UK home cooks in mind, each recipe uses accessible ingredients and provides clear, step-by-step instructions tailored to the air fryer. Alongside classic dishes, you'll find modern twists and creative ideas that will inspire you to experiment and elevate your meals.

Whether it's a family dinner, a quick weeknight meal, or an elegant spread for entertaining, this cookbook guarantees mouthwatering results every time. Dive into a world of crispy, tender, and flavourful dishes with the ease and convenience of your air fryer. Let this cookbook transform your kitchen into a haven of Italian delights. Buon appetito!

Fundamentals of an Air Fryer

What is an Air Fryer?

An air fryer is an innovative kitchen appliance designed to mimic the effects of deep frying using minimal oil—or none at all. It works by circulating hot air at high speed to cook food evenly, producing a crispy exterior and tender interior. Compact, efficient, and highly versatile, the air fryer has become a popular choice for health-conscious individuals, families, and those seeking convenient cooking solutions. By offering a healthier alternative to traditional frying methods, the air fryer revolutionises how we approach home cooking.

How Does an Air Fryer Work?

Air fryers use advanced rapid air circulation technology. A powerful fan and heating element work together to create the ideal cooking environment. Here's how it operates:

1. **Heating Element:** The element heats the air inside the appliance to a set temperature.
2. **High-Speed Fan:** A fan circulates the hot air rapidly around the food, ensuring even cooking.
3. **Crispy Results:** The intense air movement replicates the crispiness of fried food while requiring only a fraction of the oil traditionally used.

Many air fryers go beyond frying, offering additional functions such as roasting, grilling, baking, and reheating, making them a multifunctional addition to any kitchen.

Benefits of Using an Air Fryer

Reduced Oil Usage: The air fryer drastically reduces the need for oil, allowing you to create crispy, fried-like dishes with up to 90% less oil compared to traditional frying methods. This not only promotes healthier eating but also saves money on cooking oils.

Even Cooking: The rapid air circulation technology ensures consistent heat distribution, preventing hot spots and undercooked areas. This feature is particularly beneficial for cooking larger items like chicken or roasting vegetables.

Retains Nutrients: Cooking methods such as deep frying or boiling can strip foods of their natural nutrients. Air frying preserves these nutrients better, ensuring your meals are as wholesome as they are tasty.

Crispy Texture Without the Mess: Traditional frying can leave your kitchen greasy and filled with lingering odours. Air fryers eliminate messy oil splatters, keeping your kitchen clean and fresh-smelling.

Safe for Beginners: Air fryers come with built-in safety features like auto shut-off, cool-touch exteriors, and easy-to-use controls, making them ideal for new cooks or anyone nervous about handling hot oil.

Customisable Cooking Options: With adjustable temperature and time controls, you can customise the cooking process to suit specific recipes, giving you complete control over your dishes.

Perfect for Small Portions: Air fryers are great for cooking single servings or small portions, reducing food waste and making them ideal for solo cooks, students, or those with small families.

No Need to Babysit Your Food: Unlike traditional frying methods that require constant attention, air fryers allow you to set the time and temperature and walk away, freeing you up to multitask.

Energy Efficient: Air fryers consume less energy than conventional ovens or stovetops, helping to lower your energy bills while cooking your meals quickly.

Adaptable to Various Cuisines: From Asian stir-fries to Mediterranean roasted veggies, the air fryer can handle a variety of cooking styles, making it suitable for experimenting with global cuisines.

Reheats Without Soggy Results: Unlike microwaves, which can make reheated food soggy, air fryers revive leftovers with a fresh, crispy texture, bringing them back to life.

Great for Meal Prep: Preparing food in batches is easy with an air fryer, as it can handle multiple cooking functions like roasting, frying, and reheating, making meal prep more efficient.

Child-Friendly Meals: Quickly prepare healthier versions of kids' favourites like chicken nuggets, fries, or fish fingers, offering the same taste with less guilt.

Perfect for Desserts: Beyond savoury meals, air fryers are excellent for making desserts such as cakes, muffins, and even crispy churros, expanding their versatility.

Portable and Compact: Small enough to move around, air fryers are perfect for homes with limited kitchen space, dormitories, or even for use in caravans.

Less Preheating Time: Unlike traditional ovens that take time to reach the desired temperature, air fryers heat up in just minutes, saving time and effort.

Consistent Results: Thanks to precise temperature and timing controls, air fryers deliver consistent results, ensuring your food is perfectly cooked every time.

Eco-Friendly Option: Using less energy and oil makes air frying an environmentally friendlier choice, reducing both resource consumption and waste.

By combining health benefits, versatility, and ease of use, air fryers have become a staple for modern cooking, offering a smarter, cleaner, and tastier approach to mealtime.

Step-by-Step Guide to Using an Air Fryer

1. Prepare the Air Fryer
- Place your air fryer on a flat, heat-resistant surface with at least 6 inches (15 cm) of clearance around it for proper airflow.
- Ensure the appliance is clean and free of any leftover grease or food particles from previous use.
- Plug the air fryer into a suitable power socket.

2. Insert Accessories
- Place the crisper plate or basket into the designated compartment, ensuring it is securely positioned. The crisper plate allows air to circulate evenly for optimal crispness.

3. Preheat (if required)
- Check your air fryer's manual. Some models require preheating. If necessary, set the temperature to the desired level and run the air fryer for 3-5 minutes before adding your food.

4. Prepare Your Ingredients
- Wash and dry your ingredients thoroughly.
- If desired, lightly coat them with oil (e. g. , olive or sunflower oil) to enhance crispness and flavour. Use a sprayer or a small brush for even application.
- Season your ingredients with salt, spices, or marinades as per your recipe.

5. Load the Basket
- Place the ingredients in the basket or on the crisper plate in a single, even layer. Avoid overcrowding as this can hinder proper air circulation and even cooking.
- If cooking larger quantities, cook in batches for consistent results.

6. Select the Air Fry Function
- Turn the dial or press the function button to select "Air Fry" on the control panel.
- Adjust the temperature by pressing the TEMP button and setting it according to your recipe. Most air-fried foods require temperatures between 180°C and 200°C.
- Set the time using the TIME button or dial. Cooking times vary but typically range between 10-25 minutes, depending on the recipe and portion size.

7. Start Cooking
- Press the START button to begin the cooking process.
- Monitor the progress through the transparent lid (if available) or by pausing the unit and checking the food.

8. Shake or Flip Ingredients
- Halfway through cooking, pause the air fryer by pressing the START/PAUSE button.
- Remove the basket and shake it gently to redistribute the ingredients or flip them using silicone tongs for even browning.

9. Complete Cooking
- Once the timer finishes, the air fryer will beep. Some models display "COOL" during a brief cooling phase.
- Carefully remove the basket using oven mitts or heat-resistant gloves, as it will be hot.

10. Serve Immediately
Transfer the food to a serving dish using silicone or wooden utensils to avoid damaging the non-stick coating.

11. Clean the Air Fryer
- Allow the appliance to cool completely before cleaning.
- Wash the crisper plate and basket in warm, soapy water or place them in the dishwasher if they are dishwasher-safe.
- Wipe down the exterior and control panel with a damp cloth.

By following these detailed steps, you'll ensure your food is perfectly crisped and evenly cooked, every time you use the air fry function.

Frequently Asked Questions About an Air Fryer

1. Can I cook frozen foods in an air fryer?
Yes, air fryers are ideal for cooking frozen foods like chips, chicken nuggets, or fish fingers. Simply place the frozen items in the basket, adjust the temperature and cooking time, and enjoy perfectly cooked food.

2. Is it necessary to use oil in an air fryer?
Oil is optional in an air fryer. While it's not required for many foods, a small amount of oil can enhance crispiness and flavour, especially for fresh vegetables or potatoes.

3. Can I bake in an air fryer?
Yes, many air fryers can bake cakes, cookies, muffins, and bread. Be sure to use the appropriate accessories and adjust cooking times as

Fundamentals of an Air Fryer | 03

needed.

4. Are air fryers easy to clean?

Most air fryers come with removable, dishwasher-safe parts like baskets and trays. For manual cleaning, use warm, soapy water and a soft sponge to avoid scratching non-stick surfaces.

5. Can I use aluminium foil or parchment paper in an air fryer?

Yes, you can use aluminium foil or parchment paper, but ensure there is enough space for air to circulate. Avoid blocking vents or wrapping food too tightly.

6. What types of foods can I cook in an air fryer?

Air fryers are versatile and can cook a variety of foods, including chips, roasted vegetables, chicken, fish, burgers, baked goods, and even reheated leftovers.

7. How do I prevent food from sticking to the basket?

To avoid sticking, lightly coat the basket or food with a small amount of oil or use non-stick cooking spray. Shake or toss the food halfway through cooking for even results.

8. Can I cook multiple foods at the same time?

Yes, some air fryers with dual baskets or layered accessories allow you to cook multiple items simultaneously. Just ensure the cooking times and temperatures are compatible.

Fundamentals of Italian Cuisine

What is Italian Cuisine?

Italian cuisine is a culinary tradition renowned for its simplicity, elegance, and ability to bring people together. Rooted in centuries of history, it showcases regional diversity, an appreciation for high-quality ingredients, and a deep connection to community. Below is a comprehensive exploration of Italian cuisine, presented in chapters that delve into its culture, style, etiquette, signature dishes, and preparation.

Italian Food Culture

Symbol of Togetherness: Food in Italy is much more than sustenance; it is an integral part of social and cultural identity. Italians see meals as an opportunity to connect with loved ones, celebrate traditions, and enjoy the fruits of their labour. Italian meals are central to family and social life, symbolising warmth, hospitality, and shared joy.

Seasonal and Regional Focus: Menus revolve around seasonal produce and regional specialities, showcasing Italy's diverse geography and historical influences.

Leisurely Meals: Meals are often leisurely, with multiple courses enjoyed over hours. Meals are unhurried, often stretching over hours, and celebrated with traditional recipes passed through generations.

Festive Traditions: Special occasions like Christmas, Easter, and weddings are marked by elaborate feasts featuring iconic dishes. From family Sunday lunches to festive occasions like Christmas, food plays a pivotal role in uniting people. Traditional recipes, passed down through generations, reflect respect for history and heritage.

Characteristics of Italian Dishes

Italian dishes are designed to highlight the natural flavour of ingredients. Characteristics include:

- **Seasonality:** Seasonal fruits and vegetables are the cornerstone of Italian cooking.
- **Simplicity:** Recipes often involve just a few ingredients, such as pasta with olive oil, garlic, and chili (aglio e olio).
- **Balance:** Meals are designed to be well-rounded, offering a mix of carbohydrates, proteins, and vegetables.
- **Freshness:** Fresh pasta, handmade dough, and just-picked herbs are widely used.
- **Staple Dishes:** Pasta, pizza, risotto, and soups take centre stage, offering endless regional variations.
- **Balanced Courses:** Meals often include antipasto (starter), primo (pasta or risotto), secondo (main dish), and dolce (dessert).
- **Elegant Desserts:** Tiramisu and panna cotta embody indulgence with sophistication.

Italian Dining Etiquette

Italian dining etiquette reflects respect for the meal and company. Here are a few key customs:

- **Timing:** Meals are never rushed. Even coffee is savoured slowly.
- **Bread:** Bread is a staple but is not eaten as a starter. Instead, it is used to accompany the meal or soak up sauces ("fare la scarpetta").
- **Sharing:** Meals are often shared family-style, encouraging conversation and bonding.
- **Toasts:** A meal typically begins with "Salute!" to toast good health.
- **Courses:** Traditional meals include multiple courses: antipasto (starter), primo (first course, often pasta or risotto), secondo (main course, usually meat or fish), and dolce (dessert).

Italian Regional Cuisines

Italy's geography and history have resulted in a vast array of regional cuisines. Each region brings its own flavours and techniques:

- **North:** Creamy risottos, cheeses, and polenta are common in Lombardy and Piedmont.
- **Central:** Tuscany offers rustic, hearty fare like ribollita, while Rome is famous for carbonara and cacio e pepe.
- **South:** Sicily combines Mediterranean and Arab influences in dishes like arancini and caponata. Naples is the birthplace of pizza.
- **Islands:** Sardinia is known for its unique pasta, fregola, and pecorino cheeses.

How to Prepare Iconic Italian Dishes?

Pizza Margherita

A crispy base topped with tomato sauce, mozzarella, and basil, representing the Italian flag.

Ingredients:

For the Dough:

2¼ cups (280g) all-purpose flour
1 teaspoon salt
1 teaspoon sugar
1 packet (7g) dry yeast
¾ cup (180ml) warm water
1 tablespoon olive oil

For the Toppings:

½ cup (120ml) tomato sauce (preferably San Marzano tomatoes, crushed)
200g fresh mozzarella, sliced
Fresh basil leaves
2 tablespoons olive oil
Salt to taste

Step-by-Step Instructions:

Prepare the Dough: In a small bowl, dissolve the yeast and sugar in warm water. Let it sit for 5–10 minutes until frothy. In a large bowl, combine the flour and salt. Gradually add the yeast mixture and olive oil to the flour. Mix until a dough forms. Transfer the dough to a lightly floured surface and knead for about 8–10 minutes until smooth and elastic. Place the dough in a lightly oiled bowl, cover with a damp cloth, and let it rise in a warm place for 1–2 hours, or until it doubles in size.
Preheat the Oven: Preheat your oven to its highest temperature (250°C) or preheat a pizza stone if available.
Roll Out the Dough: Punch down the dough and divide it into two equal portions. Roll out one portion on a floured surface into a thin circle, about 10–12 inches in diameter.
Add the Toppings: Transfer the rolled dough onto a baking tray or pizza peel if using a pizza stone. Spread a thin layer of tomato sauce evenly across the surface, leaving a small border around the edges. Place slices of fresh mozzarella evenly on top of the sauce. Add a few fresh basil leaves. Drizzle lightly with olive oil and sprinkle a pinch of salt.
Bake the Pizza: Place the pizza in the preheated oven or on the pizza stone. Bake for 7–10 minutes, or until the crust is golden, the cheese is bubbling, and slightly browned in spots.
Serve: Remove the pizza from the oven, drizzle with a touch more olive oil if desired, and serve hot.
Enjoy this iconic and simple Italian dish, which captures the essence of fresh and bold flavours!

Spaghetti Carbonara

Creamy pasta made with eggs, Pecorino Romano, guanciale, and black pepper.

Ingredients:

400g spaghetti
150g guanciale (cured pork jowl) or pancetta, diced
3 large eggs
50g Pecorino Romano cheese, grated
50g Parmesan cheese, grated
Freshly ground black pepper
Salt (for pasta water)

Step-by-Step Instructions:

Prepare the Pasta: Bring a large pot of salted water to a boil. Cook the spaghetti until al dente according to the package instructions. Reserve about 1 cup of pasta water before draining.
Cook the Guanciale: In a large frying pan, cook the guanciale over medium heat until it is crispy and golden. Stir occasionally to ensure even cooking. Remove the pan from heat and leave the guanciale in the pan to keep warm.
Make the Sauce: In a mixing bowl, whisk together the eggs, Pecorino Romano, Parmesan, and a generous amount of black pepper until well combined. Set the mixture aside.
Combine Pasta and Guanciale: Add the drained spaghetti directly into the frying pan with the guanciale. Toss well to coat the pasta in the rendered fat.
Create the Creamy Carbonara Sauce: Remove the pan from heat (to prevent scrambling the eggs). Pour the egg and cheese mixture over the pasta and toss quickly to coat the spaghetti evenly. The residual heat will cook the eggs and create a creamy sauce. If the sauce seems too thick, add reserved pasta water a little at a time until the desired consistency is achieved.
Serve: Plate the spaghetti and sprinkle with additional Pecorino Romano and black pepper for garnish. Serve immediately, ensuring the dish remains warm.
Enjoy the rich, creamy, and authentic taste of this classic Roman dish, highlighting the simplicity and brilliance of Italian cooking!

Tiramisu

Ingredients:

300g ladyfingers (savoiardi biscuits)
500g mascarpone cheese
4 large eggs (separated into yolks and whites)
100g granulated sugar
300ml strong espresso (cooled to room temperature)
50ml coffee liqueur (optional, such as Kahlúa or Marsala wine)

Unsweetened cocoa powder (for dusting)

Step-by-Step Instructions:

Prepare the Mascarpone Cream: In a large bowl, whisk the egg yolks with the sugar until the mixture is pale and creamy. Add the mascarpone cheese to the egg yolk mixture. Whisk until smooth and well combined.

Whip the Egg Whites: In a separate clean, dry bowl, beat the egg whites until stiff peaks form. Gently fold the egg whites into the mascarpone mixture. Do this in batches, using a spatula to maintain the fluffy texture.

Prepare the Coffee Mixture: Combine the cooled espresso with the coffee liqueur (if using) in a shallow dish. Stir well and set aside.

Assemble the Tiramisu Layers:
1. Quickly dip each ladyfinger into the coffee mixture. Do not soak for too long to prevent them from becoming soggy.
2. Arrange a layer of dipped ladyfingers at the bottom of a rectangular serving dish or individual glasses.
3. Spread a layer of the mascarpone cream evenly over the ladyfingers.
4. Repeat the process, adding another layer of dipped ladyfingers and topping with mascarpone cream until the dish is full. Finish with a layer of mascarpone cream on top.

Chill and Garnish:

Cover the dish with cling film and refrigerate for at least 4 hours, or overnight for best results.

Before serving, dust the top generously with cocoa powder.

Serving Tips: Slice into portions and serve chilled. For added flair, garnish with chocolate shavings or a few coffee beans on top.

Enjoy this indulgent and iconic Italian dessert, loved for its rich, creamy layers and harmonious coffee flavours!

Risotto alla Milanese

Saffron-infused rice delivering a golden, luxurious dish.

Ingredients:

1 cup (200g) Arborio rice
2 tablespoons unsalted butter
1 tablespoon olive oil
1 small onion, finely chopped
½ cup (120ml) dry white wine
4 cups (1 litre) chicken or vegetable stock, kept warm
¼ teaspoon saffron threads
½ cup (50g) grated Parmesan cheese
Salt and freshly ground black pepper to taste
Gremolata (optional) for garnish

Step-by-Step Instructions:

Prepare the Stock: Heat the chicken or vegetable stock in a saucepan over low heat. Add the saffron threads to infuse the stock with flavour and a golden hue.

Sauté the Onion: In a large, heavy-bottomed pan, melt 1 tablespoon of butter with the olive oil over medium heat. Add the chopped onion and sauté gently until softened but not browned (about 5 minutes).

Toast the Rice: Stir in the Arborio rice, ensuring it is evenly coated with the butter and oil. Toast for 2–3 minutes, stirring constantly, until the edges of the rice grains become translucent.

Deglaze with Wine: Pour in the white wine and stir until it has mostly evaporated. This step adds depth to the flavour.

Add the Stock Gradually: Begin adding the warm saffron-infused stock one ladleful at a time, stirring continuously to prevent sticking. Allow each ladleful to be absorbed before adding the next. This process helps release the starches, creating a creamy texture.

Cook to Perfection: Continue adding stock and stirring for about 18–20 minutes, or until the rice is tender but still slightly firm to the bite (al dente). The consistency should be creamy, not runny.

Incorporate Butter and Cheese: Remove the pan from heat and stir in the remaining butter and grated Parmesan cheese. Mix until well combined and creamy.

Season and Serve: Taste and adjust with salt and freshly ground black pepper as needed. Serve immediately, optionally garnished with gremolata for added freshness.

Enjoy this luxurious dish as a standalone meal or pair it with veal or roasted vegetables for a true Italian experience!

Osso Buco

Braised veal shanks in wine and broth, served with gremolata.

Ingredients:

4 veal shanks (about 2.5cm thick, with the bone in)
Salt and freshly ground black pepper (to taste)
2 tablespoons all-purpose flour (for dusting)
3 tablespoons olive oil
2 tablespoons unsalted butter
1 medium onion (finely chopped)
1 medium carrot (finely chopped)
1 celery stalk (finely chopped)
3 garlic cloves (minced)
1 cup dry white wine
1 can (400g) diced tomatoes
1 cup beef or chicken stock
2 tablespoons tomato paste
1 teaspoon dried thyme
1 bay leaf
Zest of 1 lemon (finely grated)
2 tablespoons parsley (finely chopped, for garnish)

Step-by-Step Instructions:

Prepare the Veal Shanks: Pat the veal shanks dry with kitchen paper. Season both sides with salt and pepper, then lightly dust with flour, shaking off the excess.

Brown the Shanks: Heat olive oil and butter in a large, heavy-bottomed pan over medium heat. Add the veal shanks and sear until golden brown on all sides. This step locks in flavour. Remove the shanks and set aside.

Cook the Aromatics: In the same pan, add the onion, carrot, and celery. Sauté for about 5 minutes until softened. Stir in the minced garlic and cook for an additional minute.

Deglaze the Pan: Pour in the white wine and scrape up any browned bits from the bottom of the pan. Allow the wine to simmer for 2–3 minutes to reduce slightly.

Combine Ingredients: Stir in the diced tomatoes, tomato paste, stock, thyme, and bay leaf. Return the veal shanks to the pan, ensuring they are nestled into the sauce and covered partially with liquid.

Simmer the Dish: Cover the pan with a lid and reduce the heat to low. Simmer gently for 1.5 to 2 hours, turning the shanks occasionally, until the meat is tender and falling off the bone.

Prepare the Gremolata: Mix the lemon zest with chopped parsley in a small bowl. Set aside for garnishing.

Serve the Osso Buco: Remove the bay leaf and discard. Plate the veal shanks and spoon the sauce generously over them. Garnish with gremolata for a burst of fresh flavour.

Serving Suggestions: Serve over creamy risotto, polenta, or alongside crusty bread to soak up the rich sauce. Pair with a glass of dry white wine for a classic Italian dining experience.

Enjoy this Milanese classic with its luxurious flavours and tender texture!

Why Italian Cuisine is Timeless?

Adaptability: Recipes can be tailored to suit individual tastes and dietary needs.

Fresh Ingredients: Emphasis on quality, seasonal produce ensures exceptional flavour.

Celebration of Life: Italian meals encourage relaxation, conversation, and connection.

Global Appeal: Its mix of comfort and elegance continues to captivate food enthusiasts worldwide.

Italian cuisine is a heartfelt celebration of tradition, simplicity, and vibrant flavours, making every meal an experience to cherish. Whether enjoyed at a trattoria in Italy or recreated in your own kitchen, it remains a testament to the universal language of food.

Chapter 1 Breakfast Recipes

Breakfast Bacon Egg Cups

⏰ **Prep Time: 10 minutes**   🍲 **Cook: 8 minutes**   ≋ **Serves: 2**

Ingredients:
1 cooked bacon slice, cut into small-sized pieces
2 eggs
2 tablespoons milk
Powdered black pepper, as desired
1 teaspoon marinara sauce
1 tablespoon Parmesan cheese, grated
1 tablespoon fresh parsley, cut up

Preparation:
1. Slide the inner basket of your Air Fryer into the Air Fryer and set at 180ºC to preheat for 4-5 minutes. 2. Divide the bacon pieces into 2 ramekins. 3. Crack 1 egg in each ramekin over the bacon. 4. Pour the milk over eggs and sprinkle with black pepper. 5. Top with marinara sauce, followed by the Parmesan cheese. 6. After preheating, place the ramekins in the Air Fryer Basket. 7. Slide the basket inside and set the time for 8 minutes. 8. After the cooking period is finished, take off the ramekins from Air Fryer and sprinkle with parsley. 9. Sprinkle with parsley and enjoy right away.

Nutritional Information per Serving: Calories: 176| Fat: 11.8g| Sat Fat: 4.1g| Carbohydrates: 6.5g| Fibre: 0.4g| Sugar: 1.7g| Protein: 13.2g

Ham and Egg Bake

⏰ **Prep Time: 10 minutes**   🍲 **Cook: 12 minutes**   ≋ **Serves: 2**

Ingredients:
4 large-sized eggs, divided
Salt and powdered black pepper, as desired
2 tablespoons heavy cream
2 teaspoons unsalted butter, softened
55g ham, thinly sliced
⅛ teaspoon smoked paprika
3 tablespoons Parmesan cheese, grated
2 teaspoons fresh chives, minced

Preparation:
1. Slide the inner basket of your Air Fryer into the Air Fryer and set at 160ºC to preheat for 4-5 minutes. 2. In a bowl, put 1 egg, salt, black pepper, and cream and whisk to form a smooth mixture. 3. In the bottom of a pie dish, spread the butter. 4. Place the ham slices over the butter and top with the egg mixture. 5. Carefully, crack the remaining eggs on top and sprinkle with paprika, salt, and black pepper. 6. Top with cheese and chives. 7. After preheating, place the pie dish in the Air Fryer Basket. 8. Slide the basket inside and set the time for 12 minutes. 9. After the cooking period is finished, take off the pie dish from Air Fryer and place onto a cooling metal rack to cool for around 5 minutes before enjoying.

Nutritional Information per Serving: Calories: 306| Fat: 23.8g| Sat Fat: 11.1g| Carbohydrates: 2.7g| Fibre: 0.5g| Sugar: 0.8g| Protein: 20.5g

Tomato and Egg Bake

⏰ **Prep Time: 10 minutes**   🍲 **Cook: 20 minutes**   ≋ **Serves: 2**

Ingredients:

4 eggs
30g yellow onion, cut up
90g tomatoes, cut up
120ml unsweetened almond milk
110g Gouda cheese, shredded
Salt, as desired

Preparation:

1. Slide the inner basket of your Air Fryer into the Air Fryer and set at 170°C to preheat for 4-5 minutes. 2. In a small-sized baking pan, put the eggs and remaining ingredients and blend to incorporate. 3. After preheating, place the baking pan in the Air Fryer Basket. 4. Slide the basket inside and set the time for 20 minutes. 5. After the cooking period is finished, take off the baking pan from Air Fryer and place onto a cooling metal rack to cool for around 5 minutes before enjoying.

Nutritional Information per Serving: Calories: 227| Fat: 15.7g| Sat Fat: 6.8g| Carbohydrates: 4.8g| Fibre: 1.1g| Sugar: 2.5g| Protein: 16.9g

Spinach and Egg Ramekins

⏰ **Prep Time: 10 minutes**   🍲 **Cook: 10 minutes**   ≋ **Serves: 2**

Ingredients:

Olive oil baking spray
2 large-sized eggs
2 tablespoons half-and-half
2 tablespoons frozen spinach, thawed
4 teaspoons mozzarella cheese, grated
Salt and powdered black pepper, as desired

Preparation:

1. Slide the inner basket of your Air Fryer into the Air Fryer and set at 165°C to preheat for 4-5 minutes. 2. Spray 2 ramekins with baking spray. 3. In each ramekin, crack 1 egg. 4. Divide the half-and-half, spinach, cheese, salt, and black pepper and each ramekin and gently blend to incorporate without breaking the yolks. 5. After preheating, place the ramekins in the Air Fryer Basket. 6. Slide the basket inside and set the time for 10 minutes. 7. After the cooking period is finished, take off the ramekins from Air Fryer and place onto a cooling metal rack to cool for around 5 minutes before enjoying.

Nutritional Information per Serving: Calories: 251| 19.216.7g| Sat Fat: 8.6g| Carbohydrates: 3.1g| Fibre: 0g| Sugar: 0.4g| Protein: 22.8g

Prosciutto Egg Cups

⏰ **Prep Time: 10 minutes**   🍲 **Cook: 12 minutes**   ≋ **Serves: 4**

Ingredients:

4 slices prosciutto
30g baby spinach
4 eggs
Salt and black pepper, to taste

Preparation:

1. Set the Air Fryer at 190°C to preheat for 4-5 minutes. 2. Layer 4 ramekins using muffin cups. 3. Put one bacon slice on each ramekin and press the bacon slightly down. 4. Crack one egg inside each ramekin. Top each ramekin with spinach leaves and season with salt and black pepper. 5. After preheating, place the ramekins in the Air Fryer Basket. 6. Slide the basket inside and set the time for 12 minutes. 7. Once done, take out the ramekins and serve.

Nutritional Information per Serving: Calories: 222| Fat: 15.4g| Sat Fat: 5g| Carbohydrates: 1g| Fibre: 2g| Sugar: 0.2g| Protein: 20.6g

Smoked Trout Frittata

⏰ **Prep Time: 10 minutes**　🍲 **Cook: 20 minutes**　🍃 **Serves: 4**

Ingredients:

2 tablespoons olive oil
1 onion, sliced
6 eggs
½ tablespoon horseradish sauce
2 tablespoons crème fraiche
2 hot-smoked trout fillets, cut up
5g fresh dill, cut up

Preparation:

1. Sizzle the oil into a wok on burner at medium heat. 2. Cook the onion for around 4-5 minutes. 3. In the meantime, in a bowl, put the eggs, horseradish sauce, and crème fraiche and blend to incorporate. 4. Take off from burner and transfer the onion into a baking pan. 5. Top with the egg mixture, followed by trout and dill. 6. Slide the inner basket of your Air Fryer into the Air Fryer and set at 160°C to preheat for 4-5 minutes. 7. After preheating, place the baking pan in the Air Fryer Basket. 8. Slide the basket inside and set the time for 20 minutes. 9. After the cooking period is finished, take off the baking pan from Air Fryer and place onto a cooling metal rack to cool for around 5 minutes before enjoying.

Nutritional Information per Serving: Calories: 288| Fat: 19.2g| Sat Fat: 4.4g| Carbohydrates: 5.1g| Fibre: 1g| Sugar: 1.8g| Protein: 24.4

Sausage and Tomato Frittata

⏰ **Prep Time: 10 minutes**　🍲 **Cook: 10 minutes**　🍃 **Serves: 1**

Ingredients:

½ of Italian sausage, sliced
4 cherry tomatoes, halved
3 eggs
1 tablespoon olive oil
1-2 tablespoons Parmesan cheese, shredded
1 teaspoon fresh parsley, cut up
Salt and powdered black pepper, as desired

Preparation:

1. Slide the inner basket of your Air Fryer into the Air Fryer and set at 180°C to preheat for 4-5 minutes. 2. In a small-sized baking pan, put the sausage slices and cherry tomatoes. 3. After preheating, place the baking pan in the Air Fryer Basket. 4. Slide the basket inside and set the time for 10 minutes. 5. In the meantime, in a small-sized bowl, put the remaining ingredients and whisk to incorporate thoroughly. 6. After 5 minutes of cooking, put the egg mixture over sausage mixture. 7. After the cooking period is finished, take off the baking pan from Air Fryer and place onto a cooling metal rack to cool for around 5 minutes before enjoying.

Nutritional Information per Serving: Calories: 489| Fat: 40.6g| Sat Fat: 10.8g| Carbohydrates: 4.8g| Fibre: 1.1g| Sugar: 3.4g| Protein: 27.5g

Spinach Frittata with Tomato and Onion

⏱ Prep Time: 10 minutes   🍲 Cook: 18 minutes   🍽 Serves: 2

Ingredients:

60g half-and-half
4 large-sized eggs
Salt and powdered black pepper, as desired
50g fresh spinach, cut up
65g onion, cut up
45g tomato, cut up
60g feta cheese, crumbled

Preparation:

1. Slide the inner basket of your Air Fryer into the Air Fryer and set at 180°C to preheat for 4-5 minutes. 2. In a bowl, put the half-and-half, eggs, salt, and black pepper and whisk to incorporate thoroughly. 3. Put in the spinach, onion, tomatoes, and feta cheese and blend to incorporate. 4. Place the mixture into a baking pan. 5. After preheating, place the baking pan in the Air Fryer Basket. 6. Slide the basket inside and set the time for 18 minutes. 7. After the cooking period is finished, take off the baking pan from Air Fryer and place onto a cooling metal rack to cool for around 5 minutes before enjoying.

Nutritional Information per Serving: Calories: 304| Fat: 21.6g| Sat Fat: 10.9g| Carbohydrates: 8.3g| Fibre: 1.6g| Sugar: 4.3g| Protein: 20.2g

Oatmeal Raisin Muffins

⏱ Prep Time: 10 minutes   🍲 Cook: 10-12 minutes   🍽 Serves: 4

Ingredients:

Olive oil baking spray
60g flour
20g rolled oats
⅛ teaspoon baking powder
100g powdered sugar
115g butter, softened
2 eggs
¼ teaspoon vanilla extract
35g raisins

Preparation:

1. Slide the inner basket of your Air Fryer into the Air Fryer and set at 180°C to preheat for 4-5 minutes. 2. Spray 4 muffin molds with baking spray. 3. In a bowl, blend together the flour, oats, and baking powder. 4. In another bowl, put the sugar and butter and whisk until you get the creamy texture. 5. Put in the egg and vanilla extract and whisk to incorporate thoroughly. 6. Put the egg mixture into the oat mixture and blend until just incorporated. Fold in the raisins. 7. Place the mixture into the muffin molds. 8. After preheating, place the muffin molds in the Air Fryer Basket. 9. Slide the basket inside and set the time for 10-12 minutes. 10. After the cooking period is finished, take off the muffin molds from Air Fryer and place onto a cooling metal rack to cool for around 10 minutes. 11. Carefully, invert the muffins onto the metal rack to thoroughly cool before enjoying.

Nutritional Information per Serving: Calories: 398| Fat: 25.8g| Sat Fat: 9.9g| Carbohydrates: 37.8g| Fibre: 9.6g| Sugar: 20.4g| Protein: 5.6g

Soft Date Bread

⏲ **Prep Time: 15 minutes**   🍲 **Cook: 22 minutes**   ❧ **Serves: 8**

Ingredients:

Olive oil baking spray
370g dates, pitted and chopped
55g butter
240ml hot water
180g all-purpose flour
90g brown sugar
1 teaspoon baking powder
1 teaspoon baking soda
½ teaspoon salt
1 egg

Preparation:

1. Spray a loaf pan with baking spray. 2. In a large bowl, put the dates and butter and top with the hot water. Set it aside for around 5 minutes. 3. In a separate bowl, put the flour, brown sugar, baking powder, baking soda, and salt and blend thoroughly. 4. In the same bowl of dates, put in the flour mixture and egg and blend to incorporate thoroughly. 5. Place the mixture into the loaf pan. 6. Slide the inner basket of your Air Fryer into the Air Fryer and set at 170ºC to preheat for 4-5 minutes. 7. After preheating, place the loaf pan in the Air Fryer Basket. 8. Slide the basket inside and set the time for 22 minutes. 9. After the cooking period is finished, take off the loaf pan from Air Fryer and place onto a cooling metal rack for around 10 minutes. 10. Carefully, take out the bread from pan and put onto the metal rack to cool thoroughly. 11. Cut the bread into slices and enjoy.

Nutritional Information per Serving: Calories: 276| Fat: 5.8g| Sat Fat: 1.9g| Carbohydrates: 55.3g| Fibre: 13.6g| Sugar: 35.3g| Protein: 3.9g

Classic Cinnamon Toast

⏲ **Prep Time: 5 minutes**   🍲 **Cook: 8 minutes**   ❧ **Serves: 1**

Ingredients:

2 thick slices of whole wheat bread
1 tablespoon white sugar
½ teaspoon nutmeg
2 teaspoons butter
1 teaspoon cinnamon
2 teaspoons brown sugar

Preparation:

1. Line the inner basket of your Air Fryer with parchment paper and slide it into the Air Fryer, and set it at 200ºC to preheat for 4-5 minutes. 2. Take a medium bowl and combine cinnamon, nutmeg, brown sugar, and white sugar. 3. With a knife, evenly butter both sides of the bread slices. 4. Sprinkle the bowl mixture over both sides of bread slices. 5. After preheating, place the bread slices in an Air Fryer basket lined with parchment paper, slide the basket into the air fryer and set the time for 5 minutes. 6. Turn the bread slices halfway through. 7. Once finished, serve and enjoy.

Nutritional Information per Serving: Calories: 285| Fat: 9.9g| Sat Fat: 5.2g| Carbohydrates: 43g| Fibre: 1.1g| Sugar: 4g| Protein: 7.5g

Ham and Cheese Breakfast Casserole

⏰ **Prep Time: 5 minutes** 🍲 **Cook: 15 minutes** 🍽 **Serves: 2**

Ingredients:

1 tomato, chopped
1 tablespoon margarine
Salt and freshly ground black pepper, to taste
225g ham, chopped
2 eggs
115g cheese, shredded

Preparation:

1. Set the Air Fryer at 150ºC to preheat for 4-5 minutes. 2. Whisk the eggs in a bowl. 3. Add the salt, pepper, cheese, margarine and tomato. 4. Place a layer of ham in a round baking dish. 5. Pour the egg mixture on top of ham. 6. After preheating, place the baking pan in the Air Fryer Basket. 7. Slide the basket inside and set the time for 15 minutes. 8. When done, serve and enjoy the breakfast!

Nutritional Information per Serving: Calories: 96| Fat: 9g| Sat Fat: 1g| Carbohydrates: 10g| Fibre: 0.1g| Sugar: 0g| Protein: 35g

Kale and Cheese Omelet

⏰ **Prep Time: 5 minutes** 🍲 **Cook: 10 minutes** 🍽 **Serves: 1**

Ingredients:

Cooking spray
3 eggs, lightly beaten
3 tablespoons kale, chopped
1 tablespoon parsley, chopped
3 tablespoons cottage cheese, crumbled
1 tablespoon basil, chopped
Salt and freshly ground pepper, as desired

Preparation:

1. Spray the baking dish with cooking spray. 2. Whisk the eggs with salt and pepper in a bowl. 3. Add remaining ingredients and stir well to combine. 4. Pour the egg mixture into the greased dish. 5. Slide the inner basket of your Air Fryer into the Air Fryer and set at 165ºC to preheat for 4-5 minutes. 6. After preheating, place the baking dish in the Air Fryer Basket. 7. Slide the basket inside and set the time for 10 minutes. 8. After the cooking period is finished, take off the baking pan from the Air Fryer. 9. Serve and enjoy.

Nutritional Information per Serving: Calories: 154| Fat: 12g| Sat Fat: 3.3g| Carbohydrates: 0.6g| Fibre: 0.2g| Sugar: 0.3g| Protein: 11g

Egg in Avocado

⏰ **Prep Time: 10 minutes** 🍲 **Cook: 5 minutes** 🍽 **Serves: 2**

Ingredients:

1 large Avocado, pitted and cut in half
1 teaspoon chives
Oil spray, for greasing
⅓ teaspoon Paprika powder
2 small organic eggs
Salt and black pepper, to taste

Preparation:

1. Set the Air Fryer at 185ºC to preheat for 4-5 minutes. 2. Cut and pit the avocado in half. Then, scoop the seed and some flesh from the centre to make a cavity for an egg to sit. 3. Crack one egg on each hole of the avocado. 4. Sprinkle the paprika, salt, and black pepper on top. 5. Grease the Air Fryer Basket with oil spray. 6. After preheating, place the avocado in the greased basket. 7. Slide the basket inside and set the time for 5 minutes. 8. Once done, garnish with chives. Serve and enjoy.

Nutritional Information per Serving: Calories: 359| Fat: 30.6g| Sat Fat: 3.5g| Carbohydrates: 9.9g| Fibre: 6.7g| Sugar: 0.5g| Protein: 13.6g

Chapter 1 Breakfast Recipes | 13

Bell Pepper and Summer Squash Frittata

⏰ **Prep Time: 15 minutes** 🍳 **Cook: 20-25 minutes** 🍃 **Serves: 4**

Ingredients:

30g red bell pepper, chopped
30g yellow summer squash, chopped
2 tablespoons scallion, chopped
115g shredded Cheddar cheese, divided
5 large eggs, beaten
¼ teaspoon sea salt
2 tablespoons butter
⅛ teaspoon freshly ground black pepper

Preparation:

1. In a 7-inch baking pan, combine the summer squash, bell pepper, and scallion. Add the butter. 2. Set the Air Fryer at 175°C to preheat for 4-5 minutes. 3. After preheating, place the baking pan in the Air Fryer basket. 4. Cook the vegetables for 5 minutes or until they are crisp-tender. 5. Remove the pan from the Air Fryer. 6. In a medium bowl, whisk the eggs with the salt and black pepper. 7. Add in half of the Cheddar. 8. Add this mixture into the baking pan with the veggies. Return the pan to the Air Fryer. 9. Slide the basket inside and set the time for 10 to 15 minutes. 10. After the time is up, top the frittata using the remaining cheese. 11. Cook for another 5 minutes or until the cheese is fully melted and the frittata is set. 12. Before serving, cut into wedges and enjoy.

Nutritional Information per Serving: Calories: 260| Fat: 21g| Sat Fat: 11g| Carbohydrates: 2g| Fibre: 0.1g| Sugar: 3.02g| Protein: 15g

Cranberry Harvest Granola

⏰ **Prep Time: 10 minutes** 🍳 **Cook: 30 minutes** 🍃 **Serves: 2**

Ingredients:

40g rolled oats
120g almonds, sliced
30g pumpkin seeds
Pinch of sea salt
60g maple syrup
2 teaspoons canola oil
120g dried cranberries
Side Servings:
480ml milk

Preparation:

1. Set the Air Fryer at 150ºC to preheat for 4-5 minutes. 2. In a large bowl, add all the ingredients except for the milk. 3. Line a cake pan with parchment paper. 4. Place the bowl mixture in the cake pan. 5. After preheating, place the cake pan in the Air Fryer Basket. 6. Slide the basket inside and set the time for 30 minutes. 7. Mix the ingredients halfway through the cooking time. 8. After the cooking period is finished and the ingredients get roasted, take off the cake pan from the Air Fryer. 9. Serve with the milk. Enjoy.

Nutritional Information per Serving: Calories: 471| Fat: 20g| Sat Fat: 2.4g| Carbohydrates: 64g| Fibre: 5g| Sugar: 29g| Protein: 10g

Chapter 2 Vegetable and Side Recipes

Aubergine Parmesan

⏱ **Prep Time: 15 minutes** 🍲 **Cook: 12 minutes** ◈ **Serves: 4**

Ingredients:

1 large-sized aubergine
30g all-purpose flour
2 large-sized eggs, whisked
45g panko breadcrumbs
50g Parmesan cheese, grated,
2 teaspoons Italian seasoning
1 teaspoon garlic powder
Salt and powdered black pepper, as desired
Olive oil baking spray
250g marinara sauce
230g mozzarella cheese, thinly sliced

Preparation:

1. Cut the aubergine into ½-inch slices. 2. Sprinkle salt on both sides of the aubergine slices and put them on a metal wire rack for around 10 minutes. 3. With paper towels pat dry the aubergine slices. 4. Put the flour into a shallow dish. 5. Place the whisked eggs into a second shallow dish. 6. Put the breadcrumbs, Parmesan cheese, Italian seasoning, garlic powder, salt, and black pepper into a third shallow dish and blend thoroughly. 7. Coat each aubergine slice with flour, then dip into whisked eggs and finally coat with breadcrumb mixture. 8. Spray the aubergine slices with baking spray. 9. Spray the inner basket of your Air Fryer with baking spray and slide it into the Air Fryer. 10. Set the Air Fryer at 190ºC to preheat for 4-5 minutes. 11. After preheating, place the aubergine slices in the preheated basket of Air Fryer. 12. Slide the basket inside and set the time for 12 minutes. 13. After 10 minutes of cooking, top each aubergine slice with marinara sauce and a mozzarella cheese slice. 14. After the cooking period is finished, take off the aubergine slices from Air Fryer and enjoy moderately hot.

Nutritional Information per Serving: Calories: 30| Fat: 2.1g| Sat Fat: 0.1g| Carbohydrates: 7g| Fibre: 2.7g| Sugar: 1.3g| Protein: 1g

Parmesan Asparagus

⏱ **Prep Time: 10 minutes** 🍲 **Cook: 10 minutes** ◈ **Serves: 3**

Ingredients:

455g fresh asparagus, trimmed
1 tablespoon Parmesan cheese, grated
1 tablespoon butter, melted
1 teaspoon garlic powder
Salt and powdered black pepper, as desired
Olive oil baking spray

Preparation:

1. Spray the inner basket of your Air Fryer with baking spray and slide it into the Air Fryer. 2. Set the Air Fryer at 200ºC to preheat for 4-5 minutes. 3. In a bowl, blend together the asparagus, cheese, butter, garlic powder, salt, and black pepper. 4. After preheating, place the asparagus in the preheated basket of Air Fryer. 5. Slide the basket inside and set the time for 10 minutes. 6. After the cooking period is finished, take off the asparagus from Air Fryer and enjoy right away.

Nutritional Information per Serving: Calories: 74| Fat: 2.9g| Sat Fat: 0.1g| Carbohydrates: 7.3g| Fibre: 1.1g| Sugar: 3g| Protein: 5.2g

Brussels Sprouts with Parmesan Breadcrumbs

⏰ Prep Time: 10 minutes   🍲 Cook: 10 minutes   🍽 Serves: 3

Ingredients:

455g Brussels sprouts, trimmed and halved
1 tablespoon balsamic vinegar
1 tablespoon extra-virgin olive oil
Salt and powdered black pepper, as desired
Olive oil baking spray
110g whole wheat breadcrumbs
25g Parmesan cheese, shredded

Preparation:

1. Spray the inner basket of your Air Fryer with baking spray and slide it into the Air Fryer. 2. Set the Air Fryer at 200ºC to preheat for 4-5 minutes. 3. In a bowl, blend together the Brussels sprouts, vinegar, oil, salt, and black pepper. 4. After preheating, place the Brussels sprouts in the preheated basket of Air Fryer. 5. Slide the basket inside and set the time for 10 minutes. 6. After 5 minutes of cooking, turn the Brussels sprouts. Sprinkle the Brussels sprouts with breadcrumbs, followed by the cheese. 7. After the cooking period is finished, take off the Brussels sprouts from Air Fryer and enjoy right away.

Nutritional Information per Serving: Calories: 157| Fat: 7.2g| Sat Fat: 2g| Carbohydrates: 18.7g| Fibre: 6.3g| Sugar: 3.4g| Protein: 8.7g

Cheesy Spinach Stuffed Pasta Shells

⏰ Prep Time: 15 minutes   🍲 Cook: 20-25 minutes   🍽 Serves: 2

Ingredients:

6 uncooked jumbo pasta shells
55g mozzarella cheese, shredded and divided
30g Asiago cheese, shredded
60g ricotta cheese
60g cottage cheese
95g frozen chopped spinach, thawed and squeezed
1 tablespoon fresh chives, minced
60g meatless spaghetti sauce
Olive oil baking spray

Preparation:

1. Cook the pasta shells into a large-sized pot of salted boiling water for around 8-10 minutes. 2. Drain the pasta shells. 3. Put 30g of mozzarella cheese, Asiago cheese, ricotta cheese, cottage cheese, spinach, and chives into a small-sized bowl and blend to incorporate. 4. Stuff the pasta shells with cheese mixture. 5. Spray a baking pan with biking spray. 6. Spread 125g spaghetti sauce into the baking pan. 7. Arrange the pasta shells over the spaghetti sauce. 8. Top with the remaining spaghetti sauce and mozzarella cheese. 9. Spray the inner basket of your Air Fryer with baking spray and then slide it in the Air Fryer. 10. Set the Air Fryer at 160ºC to preheat for 4-5 minutes. 11. After preheating, place the baking pan in the preheated basket of Air Fryer. 12. Slide the basket back into the Air Fryer and set the time for 20-25 minutes. 13. After the cooking period is finished, take off the baking pan from Air Fryer and enjoy right away.

Nutritional Information per Serving: Calories: 378| Fat: 14. 4g| Sat Fat: 8. 9g| Carbohydrates: 39. 7g| Fibre: 13. 4g| Sugar: 4g| Protein: 24. 9g

Roasted Spinach with Feta

Prep Time: 10 minutes　Cook: 15 minutes　Serves: 6

Ingredients:

910g fresh spinach, cut up
1 clove garlic, minced
1 jalapeño pepper, minced
4 tablespoons butter, melted
Salt and powdered black pepper, as desired
120g feta cheese, crumbled
1 teaspoon fresh lemon zest, grated
Olive oil baking spray

Preparation:

1. Spray the inner basket of your Air Fryer with baking spray and slide it into the Air Fryer. 2. Set the Air Fryer at 170ºC to preheat for 4-5 minutes. 3. In a bowl, put the spinach, garlic, jalapeño, butter, salt, and black pepper and blend to incorporate. 4. After preheating, place the spinach mixture in the preheated basket of Air Fryer. 5. Slide the basket inside and set the time for 15 minutes. 6. After the cooking period is finished, take off the spinach mixture from Air Fryer and place into a bowl. 7. Immediately blend in the cheese and lemon zest. 8. Enjoy right away.

Nutritional Information per Serving: Calories: Calories: 170| Fat: 13.6g| Sat Fat: 8.7g| Carbohydrates: 6.9g| Fibre: 3.4g| Sugar: 1.8g| Protein: 8g

Parmesan Roasted Cauliflower

Prep Time: 10 minutes　Cook: 15 minutes　Serves: 6

Ingredients:

1 medium-sized head cauliflower
75g sour cream
25g Parmesan cheese, shredded
1 teaspoon garlic, minced
Salt and powdered black pepper, as desired
Olive oil baking spray

Preparation:

1. Spray the inner basket of your Air Fryer with baking spray and slide it into the Air Fryer. 2. Set the Air Fryer at 175ºC to preheat for 4-5 minutes. 3. With a knife, cut an X into the cauliflower head, slicing about halfway down. 4. In a small-sized bowl, put the sour cream, Parmesan, garlic, salt, and pepper and blend to incorporate. 5. Spread Parmesan mixture over the cauliflower head. 6. After preheating, place the cauliflower head in the preheated basket of Air Fryer. 7. Slide the basket inside and set the time for 15 minutes. 8. After the cooking period is finished, take off the cauliflower head from Air Fryer and transfer to a platter. 9. Cut into serving portions and enjoy.

Nutritional Information per Serving: Calories: 64| Fat: 6g| Sat Fat: 3g| Carbohydrates: 8.3g| Fibre: 1.6g| Sugar: 1g| Protein: 2g

Roasted Courgette and Squash

⏱ **Prep Time: 10 minutes**   🍳 **Cook: 10 minutes**   ❖ **Serves: 4**

Ingredients:

2 large-sized yellow squash, cut into slices
2 large-sized courgette, cut into slices
60ml olive oil
½ onion, sliced
¾ teaspoon Italian seasoning
½ teaspoon garlic salt
¼ teaspoon Seasoned salt
Olive oil baking spray

Preparation:

1. Spray the inner basket of your Air Fryer with baking spray and slide it into the Air Fryer. 2. Set the Air Fryer at 200ºC to preheat for 4-5 minutes. 3. In a large-sized bowl, blend together all the ingredients except baking spray. 4. After preheating, place the veggie mixture in the preheated basket of Air Fryer. 5. Slide the basket inside and set the time for 10 minutes. 6. After the cooking period is finished, take off the veggie mixture from Air Fryer and enjoy right away.

Nutritional Information per Serving: Calories: 106| Fat: 7.6g| Sat Fat: 1.2g| Carbohydrates: 6.9g| Fibre: 2.1g| Sugar: 3.2g| Protein: 2.2g

Roasted Ratatouille

⏱ **Prep Time: 15 minutes**   🍳 **Cook: 15 minutes**   ❖ **Serves: 4**

Ingredients:

Olive oil baking spray
1 green bell pepper, seeded and cut up
1 yellow bell pepper, seeded and cut up
1 aubergine, cut up
1 courgette, cut up
3 tomatoes, cut up
2 small-sized onions, cut up
2 cloves garlic, minced
2 tablespoons Herbs de Provence
1 tablespoon olive oil
1 tablespoon balsamic vinegar
Salt and powdered black pepper, as desired

Preparation:

1. Slide the inner basket of your Air Fryer into the Air Fryer and set at 180ºC to preheat for 4-5 minutes. 2. Spray a baking pan with baking spray. 3. In a large-sized bowl, put the vegetables, garlic, Herbs de Provence, oil, vinegar, salt, and black pepper and toss to coat well. 4. Transfer vegetable mixture into a greased baking pan. 5. After preheating, place the baking pan in the Air Fryer Basket. 6. Slide the basket inside and set the time for 15 minutes. 7. After the cooking period is finished, take off the baking pan from Air Fryer and enjoy right away.

Nutritional Information per Serving: Calories: 119| Fat: 4.2g| Sat Fat: 0.6g| Carbohydrates: 21.3g| Fibre: 7.3g| Sugar: 11.2g| Protein: 3.6g

Stuffed Bell Peppers

⏰ **Prep Time: 10 minutes** 🍲 **Cook: 16 minutes** 🍃 **Serves: 4**

Ingredients:

½ of small-sized bell pepper, seeded and cut up
1 (425g) can diced tomatoes with juice
1 (425g) can red kidney beans, rinsed and drained
175g cooked rice
1½ teaspoons Italian seasoning
4 large-sized bell peppers, tops removed and seeded
55g mozzarella cheese, shredded
1 tablespoon Parmesan cheese, grated
Olive oil baking spray

Preparation:

1. Spray the inner basket of your Air Fryer with baking spray and slide it into the Air Fryer. 2. Set the Air Fryer at 180ºC to preheat for 4-5 minutes. 3. In a bowl, blend together the cut up bell pepper, tomatoes with juice, beans, rice, and Italian seasoning. 4. Stuff each bell pepper with the rice mixture. 5. After preheating, place the bell peppers in the preheated basket of Air Fryer. 6. Slide the basket inside and set the time for 16 minutes. 7. In the meantime, in a bowl, blend together the mozzarella and Parmesan cheese. 8. After 12 minutes of cooking, top each bell pepper with cheese mixture. 9. After the cooking period is finished, take off the bell peppers from Air Fryer and enjoy moderately hot.

Nutritional Information per Serving: Calories: 394| Fat: 23.6g| Sat Fat: 10.9g| Carbohydrates: 2.6g| Fibre: 0.6g| Sugar: 10.3g| Protein: 23.2g

Homemade Pita Pizza

⏰ **Prep Time: 10 minutes** 🍲 **Cook: 5 minutes** 🍃 **Serves: 1**

Ingredients:

2 tablespoons marinara sauce
1 whole-wheat pita bread
15g fresh baby spinach leaves
½ of small-sized plum tomato, cut into 4 slices
½ of clove garlic, thinly sliced
14g part-skim mozzarella cheese, shredded
½ tablespoon Parmesan cheese, shredded
Olive oil baking spray

Preparation:

1. Spray the inner basket of your Air Fryer with baking spray and slide it into the Air Fryer. 2. Set the Air Fryer at 175ºC to preheat for 4-5 minutes. 3. Arrange the pita bread onto a plate. 4. Spread marinara sauce over 1 side of each pita bread. 5. Top with the spinach leaves, followed by tomato slices, garlic, and cheeses. 6. After preheating, place the pizza in the preheated basket of Air Fryer. 7. Slide the basket inside and set the time for 5 minutes. 8. After the cooking period is finished, take off the pizza from Air Fryer and enjoy moderately hot.

Nutritional Information per Serving: Calories: 266| Fat: 6.3g| Sat Fat: 2.7g| Carbohydrates: 42.3g| Fibre: 6.6g| Sugar: 4.5g| Protein: 12.2g

Quick Fingerling Potatoes

⏲ **Prep Time: 5 minutes** 🍲 **Cook: 15 minutes** 🍴 **Serves: 4**

Ingredients:

455g fingerling potatoes, halved
1 tablespoon olive oil
½ tablespoon garlic powder
½ tablespoon parsley flakes
Salt and black pepper, to taste Fingerling
½ tablespoon paprika

Preparation:

1. Set the Air Fryer at 170ºC to preheat for 4-5 minutes. 2. Place the potatoes in a mixing bowl. Add the garlic, oil, paprika, salt, parsley, and pepper. Stir until well combined. 3. After preheating, put the potatoes in your Air Fryer basket and cook for around 10 minutes. 4. Stir after 10 minutes and cook for an additional 5 minutes. 5. Once done, serve and enjoy.

Nutritional Information per Serving: Calories: 119| Fat: 4g| Sat Fat: 0.8g| Carbohydrates: 18g| Fibre: 3g| Sugar: 1g| Protein: 2.4g

Pesto Gnocchi

⏲ **Prep Time: 5 minutes** 🍲 **Cook: 20 minutes** 🍴 **Serves: 4**

Ingredients:

1 (455g) package shelf-stable gnocchi
1 tablespoon extra-virgin olive oil
1 medium-sized onion, chopped
1 jar (225g) pesto
35g Parmesan cheese, grated
3 garlic cloves, minced
Salt and black pepper, to taste

Preparation:

1. Set the Air Fryer at 170ºC to preheat for 4-5 minutes. 2. Combine the garlic, onion, and gnocchi in the baking pan and sprinkle with olive oil, salt, and pepper. Stir to mix. 3. After preheating, place the baking pan in the Air Fryer Basket. 4. Cook for around 15-20 minutes, stirring a few times while cooking until gnocchi are slightly browned and crisp. 5. Stir in the Parmesan cheese and pesto and serve immediately.

Nutritional Information per Serving: Calories: 330| Fat: 19g| Sat Fat: 4.2g| Carbohydrates: 55g| Fibre: 2.7g| Sugar: 1g| Protein: 13g

Herbed Mushrooms with White Wine

⏲ **Prep Time: 10 minutes** 🍲 **Cook: 30 minutes** 🍴 **Serves: 6**

Ingredients:

1 tablespoon butter
2 teaspoons Herbs de Provence
½ teaspoon garlic powder
910g fresh mushrooms
2 tablespoons white wine

Preparation:

1. Slide the inner basket of your Air Fryer into the Air Fryer and set at 150ºC to preheat for 4-5 minutes. 2. In a baking pan, blend together the butter, Herbs de Provence, and garlic powder. 3. Put in the mushrooms and blend to incorporate. 4. After preheating, place the baking pan in the Air Fryer Basket. 5. Slide the basket inside and set the time for 30 minutes. 6. After 25 minutes of cooking, blend the wine with mushroom mixture. 7. After the cooking period is finished, take off the baking pan from Air Fryer and enjoy right away.

Nutritional Information per Serving: Calories: 64| Fat: 2.6g| Sat Fat: 0.1g| Carbohydrates: 6.3g| Fibre: 1.6g| Sugar: 2.7g| Protein: 4.9g

Mixed Veggies Pancakes

⏰ **Prep Time: 15 minutes** 🍲 **Cook: 15 minutes** ≋ **Serves: 2**

Ingredients:

3 medium russet potatoes, shredded and squeezed
85g frozen peas, thawed and drained
4 tablespoons ground flaxseed
1 small onion, shredded and squeezed
55g carrots, chopped
120ml water
75g peas
40g corn, drained
5g finely chopped fresh coriander
Salt and black pepper, to taste
60g unbleached all-purpose flour
Oil spray for greasing

Preparation:

1. Line the Air Fryer basket with parchment paper and grease with oil spray. 2. Preheat the Air Fryer at 200ºC for 4-5 minutes. 3. In a large bowl, mix the flaxseed with water, and add the peas, shredded potatoes, carrots, onions, and corn. Mix everything well. 4. Add in the coriander and flour and season with salt and black pepper. 5. Make a batter for pancakes. 6. After preheating, scoop this mixture in the shape of patties on the basket lined with parchment paper. 7. Cook in batches for around 15 minutes, flipping halfway through. 8. Once all pancakes are cooked, serve and enjoy.

Nutritional Information per Serving: Calories: 170| Fat: 6g| Sat Fat: 1g| Carbohydrates: 26g| Fibre: 2g| Sugar: 1g| Protein: 6g

Roasted Root Vegetable Medley

⏰ **Prep Time: 10 minutes** 🍲 **Cook: 20 minutes** ≋ **Serves: 4**

Ingredients:

2 carrots, sliced
2 tablespoons tomato pesto
1 rutabaga, peeled and cut into chunks
1 beet, peeled and cut into chunks
2 potatoes, peeled and cut into chunks
Salt and black pepper to taste
2 tablespoons fresh thyme, chopped
1 turnip, peeled and cut into chunks
2 tablespoons olive oil

Preparation:

1. Preheat the Air Fryer at 200ºC for 4-5 minutes. 2. Combine all the root vegetables, pepper, salt, and olive oil in a bowl. Toss to mix well. 3. After preheating, transfer the vegetables to Air Fryer basket. 4. Cook for 2 minutes, then shake and proceed to cook for another 10 minutes. 5. Once cooked, combine the pesto with 2 tablespoons water, drizzle over the vegetables, and toss to coat well. 6. Sprinkle with thyme to serve.

Nutritional Information per Serving: Calories: 175| Fat: 7g| Sat Fat: 1.5g| Carbohydrates: 16g| Fibre: 3g| Sugar: 4g| Protein: 5g

Stuffed Tomatoes

⏱ **Prep Time: 15 minutes** 🍲 **Cook: 10-12 minutes** ❖ **Serves: 2**

Ingredients:

4 large tomatoes
120g panko breadcrumbs
85g mozzarella cheese, shredded and divided
6-8 fresh basil leaves, cut up
Salt and ground black pepper, as desired
Olive oil baking spray

Preparation:

1. Carefully cut off the top of each tomato and scoop out pulp and seeds. 2. Place the tomatoes onto paper towels, cut side down. Set aside for around 20 minutes. 3. Chop the tomato pulp in put into a bowl. 4. Put in the panko, 55g of mozzarella, basil, salt, and pepper and blend to incorporate. 5. Stuff the tomatoes with the panko mixture and then top each with remaining mozzarella. 6. Spray the inner basket of your Air Fryer with baking spray and then slide it in the Air Fryer. 7. Set the Air Fryer at 175ºC to preheat for 4-5 minutes. 8. After preheating, place the tomatoes in the preheated basket of Air Fryer. 9. Slide the basket back into the Air Fryer and set the time for 10-12 minutes. 10. After the cooking period is finished, take off the tomatoes from Air Fryer and enjoy right away.

Nutritional Information per Serving: Calories: 195| Fat: 9. 1g| Sat Fat: 1. 8g| Carbohydrates: 12. 7g| Fibre: 1g| Sugar: 0. 5g| Protein: 12. 9g

Healthy Courgette Fritters

⏱ **Prep Time: 15 minutes** 🍲 **Cook: 6-7 minutes** ❖ **Serves: 4**

Ingredients:

300g courgette, grated and squeezed
200g Halloumi cheese
30g all-purpose flour
2 eggs
1 teaspoon fresh dill, minced
Salt and ground black pepper, as desired

Preparation:

1. Put the courgette and remaining ingredients into a large-sized bowl and blend to incorporate thoroughly. 2. Make small-sized fritters from the mixture. 3. Spray a baking pan with baking spray. 4. Arrange the fritters into the baking pan. 5. Spray the inner basket of your Air Fryer with baking spray and then slide it in the Air Fryer. 6. Set the Air Fryer at 180ºC to preheat for 4-5 minutes. 7. After preheating, place the baking pan in the preheated basket of Air Fryer. 8. Slide the basket back into the Air Fryer and set the time for 6-7 minutes. 9. After the cooking period is finished, take off the baking pan from Air Fryer and enjoy right away. 10. Enjoy moderately hot.

Nutritional Information per Serving: Calories: 250| Fat: 15. 4g| Sat Fat: 5. 8g| Carbohydrates: 10. 7g| Fibre: 1. 2g| Sugar: 1. 5g| Protein: 13. 9g

Cherry Tomato Pasta

⏰ **Prep Time: 15 minutes** 🍲 **Cook: 12 minutes** 🍂 **Serves: 2**

Ingredients:

170g cherry tomatoes, halved
1 tablespoon olive oil
2 cloves garlic, minced
½ teaspoon mixed dried Italian herbs
3 tablespoons heavy cream
25g grated Parmesan cheese, grated
141g pasta
1 tablespoon fresh basil, cut up
Salt and ground black pepper, as desired
Olive oil baking spray

Preparation:

1. Put the tomatoes, oil, garlic, herbs, salt, and pepper into a bowl and toss to incorporate. 2. Place the tomatoes into a cake pan. 3. Spray the inner basket of your Air Fryer with baking spray and then slide it in the Air Fryer. 4. Set the Air Fryer at 180ºC to preheat for 4-5 minutes. 5. After preheating, place the cake pan in the preheated basket of Air Fryer. 6. Slide the basket back into the Air Fryer and set the time for 11 minutes. 7. After 9 minutes of cooking, put the cheese and cream into the pan and blend. 8. In the meantime, cook the pasta into a large-sized pot of salted boiling water for around 8-10 minutes. 9. Drain the pasta thoroughly. 10. After the cooking period is finished, take off the cake pan from Air Fryer and immediately blend in the pasta and basil. 11. Enjoy right away.

Nutritional Information per Serving: Calories: 446| Fat: 19. 4g| Sat Fat: 7. 8g| Carbohydrates: 53. 7g| Fibre: 3g| Sugar: 3. 5g| Protein: 13. 9g

Tomato Pizza with Courgette

⏰ **Prep Time: 15 minutes** 🍲 **Cook: 7 minutes** 🍂 **Serves: 3**

Ingredients:

225g pizza dough
1 tablespoon all-purpose flour
1 tablespoon olive oil, divided
Olive oil baking spray
115g fresh mozzarella cheese, sliced
2 medium tomatoes, thinly sliced
½ of courgette, thinly sliced
2 cloves garlic minced
Salt, as desired

Preparation:

1. Cut the pizza dough in half. 2. Spray the inner basket of your Air Fryer with baking spray and then slide it in the Air Fryer. 3. Set the Air Fryer at 190ºC to preheat for 4-5 minutes. 4. After preheating, place the pizza dough in the preheated basket of Air Fryer, oil side downwards. 5. Slide the basket back into the Air Fryer and set the time for 3 minutes. 6. After the cooking period is finished, take off the dough from Air Fryer and place onto a platter. 7. Place mozzarella over the crust, followed by the tomato, courgette, and garlic. 8. Drizzle with the remaining oil and then sprinkle with the salt. 9. Again, set the Air Fryer at 190ºC to preheat for 4-5 minutes. 10. After preheating, place the pizza in the preheated basket of Air Fryer. 11. Slide the basket back into the Air Fryer and set the time for 4 minutes. 12. After the cooking period is finished, take off the dough from Air Fryer and enjoy right away.

Nutritional Information per Serving: Calories: 558| Fat: 23. 4g| Sat Fat: 8. 8g| Carbohydrates: 65. 7g| Fibre: 3. 4g| Sugar: 11. 5g| Protein: 23. 9g

Chapter 3 Snack & Appetizer Recipes

Strawberry Bruschetta

⏰ Prep Time: 10 minutes   🍲 Cook: 4 minutes   🍽 Serves: 4

Ingredients:

4 baguette slices
1 teaspoon olive oil
Olive oil baking spray
225g mascarpone cheese, softened
2 tablespoons honey
4-5 medium-sized strawberries, hulled and sliced
2 teaspoons balsamic glaze

Preparation:

1. Spray the inner basket of your Air Fryer with baking spray and slide it into the Air Fryer. 2. Set the Air Fryer at 175ºC to preheat for 4-5 minutes. 3. Lightly brush each baguette slice with oil. 4. After preheating, place the baguette slices in the preheated basket of Air Fryer. 5. Slide the basket inside and set the time for 3-4 minutes. 6. After the cooking period is finished, take off the baguette slices from Air Fryer and place onto a platter. Set aside to cool slightly. 7. In a small-sized bowl, put the mascarpone cheese, honey, and a pinch of salt and blend to form a smooth mixture. 8. Spread the mascarpone mixture on each baguette slice. 9. Top with the strawberries and drizzle with balsamic glaze. 10. Enjoy right away.

Nutritional Information per Serving: Calories: 150| Fat: 9.6g| Sat Fat: 5g| Carbohydrates: 14.3g| Fibre: 1g| Sugar: 5g| Protein: 3.2g

Tasty Arancini

⏰ Prep Time: 15 minutes   🍲 Cook: 10 minutes   🍽 Serves: 4

Ingredients:

450g cooked risotto
35g Parmesan cheese, grated
1 egg, whisked
85g mozzarella cheese, cubed
80g breadcrumbs
Olive oil baking spray

Preparation:

1. Spray the inner basket of your Air Fryer with baking spray and slide it into the Air Fryer. 2. Set the Air Fryer at 200ºC to preheat for 4-5 minutes. 3. In a bowl, blend together the risotto, Parmesan cheese, and egg. 4. Make small-sized balls from the mixture. 5. Insert a mozzarella cube in the centre of each ball and using your fingers, smooth the risotto mixture to cover the mozzarella. 6. In a shallow dish, put the breadcrumbs. 7. Coat the balls with breadcrumbs. 8. After preheating, place the balls in the preheated basket of Air Fryer. 9. Slide the basket inside and set the time for 10 minutes. 10. After the cooking period is finished, take off the balls from Air Fryer and enjoy moderately hot.

Nutritional Information per Serving: Calories: 241| Fat: 5.2g| Sat Fat: 2.5g| Carbohydrates: 36.9g| Fibre: 0.9g| Sugar: 0.9g| Protein: 10.7g

Pizza Toast

⏰ **Prep Time: 10 minutes** 🍲 **Cook: 5-6 minutes** 🍽 **Serves: 4**

Ingredients:

4 whole-grain bread slices
120g Pizza sauce
30g mozzarella cheese, shredded
Olive oil baking spray

Preparation:

1. Spray the inner basket of your Air Fryer with baking spray and slide it into the Air Fryer. 2. Set the Air Fryer at 175ºC to preheat for 4-5 minutes. 3. Spread a layer of pizza sauce over one side of each bread slice. 4. Sprinkle each with mozzarella cheese. 5. After preheating, place the bread slices in the preheated basket of Air Fryer. 6. Slide the basket inside and set the time for 5-6 minutes. 7. After the cooking period is finished, take off the bread slices from Air Fryer and enjoy moderately hot.

Nutritional Information per Serving: Calories: 104| Fat: 3.1g| Sat Fat: 1g| Carbohydrates: 15.3g| Fibre: 2g| Sugar: 3g| Protein: 5g

Cheesy Broccoli Bites

⏰ **Prep Time: 15 minutes** 🍲 **Cook: 12 minutes** 🍽 **Serves: 10**

Ingredients:

200g broccoli florets
2 eggs, whisked
140g mozzarella cheese, grated
25g Parmesan cheese, grated
105g panko breadcrumbs
Salt and powdered black pepper, as desired
Olive oil baking spray

Preparation:

1. In a food processor, put the broccoli and process until finely crumbled. 2. In a large-sized bowl, put the broccoli with the remaining ingredients except baking spray and blend to incorporate. 3. Make small-sized balls from the mixture. 4. Arrange the balls in a baking tray and put into your fridge for at least 30 minutes. 5. Spray the inner basket of your Air Fryer with baking spray and slide it into the Air Fryer. 6. Set the Air Fryer at 175ºC to preheat for 4-5 minutes. 7. After preheating, place the balls in the preheated basket of Air Fryer. 8. Slide the basket inside and set the time for 12 minutes. 9. After the cooking period is finished, take off the balls from Air Fryer and enjoy moderately hot.

Nutritional Information per Serving: Calories: 122| Fat: 6.8g| Sat Fat: 3.8g| Carbohydrates: 3.1g| Fibre: 0.5g| Sugar: 0.5g| Protein: 6.2g

Italian Parmesan Tomato Crisps

⏰ **Prep Time: 5 minutes** 🍲 **Cook: 10 minutes** 🍽 **Serves: 4**

Ingredients:

4 Roma tomatoes, sliced
1 teaspoon Italian seasoning mix
4 tablespoons Parmesan cheese, grated
2 tablespoons olive oil
Sea salt and white pepper, to taste
Nonstick cooking oil

Preparation:

1. Generously grease the Air Fryer basket with nonstick cooking oil. 2. Set the Air Fryer at 175ºC to preheat for 4-5 minutes. 3. Toss the sliced tomatoes with the rest of the ingredients. 4. After preheating, place the tomatoes in the Air Fryer basket without overlapping. 5. Cook for around 5 minutes. Shake the basket and cook for an additional 5 minutes. Cook in batches if necessary. 6. Serve with Mediterranean aioli for dipping, if liked. 7. Serve and enjoy.

Nutritional Information per Serving: Calories: 150| Fat: 10g| Sat Fat: 7g| Carbohydrates: 2g| Fibre: 0.4g| Sugar: 0.5g| Protein: 13g

Chapter 3 Snack & Appetizer Recipes

Crispy Fried Ravioli

⏰ **Prep Time: 15 minutes** 🍳 **Cook: 10 minutes** 🍽 **Serves: 4**

Ingredients:

455g frozen ravioli
240g all-purpose flour
3 large-sized eggs
220g breadcrumbs
25g Parmesan cheese, grated
1 teaspoon Italian seasoning
1 teaspoon onion powder
1 teaspoon garlic powder
½ teaspoon salt
Olive oil baking spray

Preparation:

1. Spray the inner basket of your Air Fryer with baking spray and slide it into the Air Fryer. 2. Set the Air Fryer at 175ºC to preheat for 4-5 minutes. 3. In a bowl, put the flour. 4. In a second bowl, crack whisk the eggs. 5. In a third bowl, put the breadcrumbs, Parmesan cheese, Italian seasoning, and spices. 6. Coat the ravioli with flour, then dip into whisked eggs and finally coat with breadcrumb mixture. 7. After preheating, place the ravioli in the preheated basket of Air Fryer. 8. Slide the basket inside and set the time for 10 minutes. 9. While cooking, turn the ravioli once halfway through. 11. After the cooking period is finished, take off the ravioli from Air Fryer and enjoy moderately hot.

Nutritional Information per Serving: Calories: 220| Fat: 9.6g| Sat Fat: 3.2g| Carbohydrates: 24.3g| Fibre: 2.1g| Sugar: 1g| Protein: 11.2g

Mini Portobello Mushroom Pizza

⏰ **Prep Time: 10 minutes** 🍳 **Cook: 6 minutes** 🍽 **Serves: 2**

Ingredients:

2 Portobello mushroom caps, stemmed
2 tablespoons olive oil
⅛ teaspoon dried Italian seasoning
Salt, as desired
2 tablespoons canned tomatoes, cut up
2 tablespoons mozzarella cheese, shredded
2 Kalamata olives, pitted and sliced
Olive oil baking spray
2 tablespoons Parmesan cheese, grated
1 teaspoon red pepper flakes, crushed

Preparation:

1. Spray the inner basket of your Air Fryer with baking spray and slide it into the Air Fryer. 2. Set the Air Fryer at 160ºC to preheat for 4-5 minutes. 3. With a spoon, scoop out the centre of each mushroom cap. 4. Coat each mushroom cap with oil from both sides. 5. Sprinkle the inside of caps with Italian seasoning and salt. 6. Place the canned tomato over both caps, followed by the olives and mozzarella cheese. 7. After preheating, place the mushroom caps in the preheated basket of Air Fryer. 8. Slide the basket inside and set the time for 5-6 minutes. 9. After the cooking period is finished, take off the mushroom caps from Air Fryer and immediately sprinkle with the Parmesan cheese and red pepper flakes. 10. Enjoy right away.

Nutritional Information per Serving: Calories: 251| Fat: 21.6g| Sat Fat: 10.9g| Carbohydrates: 6.3g| Fibre: 1.1g| Sugar: 40.7| Protein: 14.2g

| Chapter 3 Snack & Appetizer Recipes

Pesto Stuffed Tomatoes

⏱ **Prep Time: 15 minutes**   🍳 **Cook: 10 minutes**   ❄ **Serves: 3**

Ingredients:

3 large-sized tomatoes, cut in half
110g breadcrumbs
25g Parmesan cheese, grated
1 teaspoon garlic, minced
1 tablespoon olive oil
½ teaspoon dried basil
½ teaspoon dried parsley
½ teaspoon dried dill
1 teaspoon salt
½ teaspoon black pepper
Olive oil baking spray

Preparation:

1. Spray the inner basket of your Air Fryer with baking spray and slide it into the Air Fryer. 2. Set the Air Fryer at 165ºC to preheat for 4-5 minutes. 3. In a small-sized bowl, put the breadcrumbs, Parmesan cheese, garlic, oil, dried herbs, salt, and black pepper and blend to incorporate. 4. Top each tomato half with breadcrumb mixture. 5. After preheating, place the tomato halves in the preheated basket of Air Fryer. 6. Slide the basket inside and set the time for 10 minutes. 7. After the cooking period is finished, take off the tomato halves from Air Fryer and enjoy.

Nutritional Information per Serving: Calories: 127| Fat: 5.6g| Sat Fat: 1g| Carbohydrates: 17.6g| Fibre: 2g| Sugar: 4.1g| Protein: 20.2g

Spanakopita Rolls

⏱ **Prep Time: 20 minutes**   🍳 **Cook: 4-5 minutes**   ❄ **Serves: 6**

Ingredients:

1 (455g) package frozen spinach, thawed
1 onion, cut up
60g fresh parsley, cut up
25g fresh mint leaves, cut up
1 egg
120g feta cheese, crumbled
40g Romano cheese, grated
¼ teaspoon powdered cardamom
Salt and powdered black pepper, as desired
1 package frozen filo dough, thawed
2 tablespoons olive oil
Olive oil baking spray

Preparation:

1. In a food processor, put the spinach and remaining ingredients except for filo dough, oil, and baking spray and process to form a smooth mixture. 2. Place 1 filo sheet on the chopping board and cut into three rectangular strips. 3. Brush each strip with the oil. 4. Add about 1 teaspoon of spinach mixture along with the short side of a strip. 5. Roll the dough to secure the filling. 6. Repeat with the remaining filo sheets and spinach mixture. 7. Spray the inner basket of your Air Fryer with baking spray and slide it into the Air Fryer. 8. Set the Air Fryer at 180ºC to preheat for 4-5 minutes. 9. After preheating, place the rolls in the preheated basket of Air Fryer. 10. Slide the basket inside and set the time for 4-5 minutes. 11. After the cooking period is finished, take off the rolls from Air Fryer and enjoy moderately hot.

Nutritional Information per Serving: Calories: 411| Fat: 18.4g| Sat Fat: 7.2g| Carbohydrates: 47.3g| Fibre: 4.9g| Sugar: 2.4g| Protein: 15.7g

Crispy Mozzarella Sticks

⏱ **Prep Time: 15 minutes**   🍲 **Cook: 12 minutes**   ≋ **Serves: 4**

Ingredients:

30g white flour
1 egg
1½ tablespoons milk
55g plain breadcrumbs
225g Mozzarella cheese block, cut into 3x½-inch sticks
Olive oil baking spray

Preparation:

1. In a shallow dish, put the flour. 2. In a second dish, blend together the eggs and milk. 3. In a third dish, put the breadcrumbs. 4. Coat the Mozzarella sticks with flour, then dip into egg mixture, and finally coat with the breadcrumbs. 5. Arrange the Mozzarella sticks onto a baking tray and freeze for around 1-2 hours. 6. Spray the inner basket of your Air Fryer with baking spray and slide it into the Air Fryer. 7. Set the Air Fryer at 200ºC to preheat for 4-5 minutes. 8. After preheating, place the Mozzarella sticks in the preheated basket of Air Fryer. 9. Slide the basket inside and set the time for 12 minutes. 10. While cooking, turn the Mozzarella sticks once halfway through. 11. After the cooking period is finished, take off the Mozzarella sticks from Air Fryer and enjoy moderately hot.

Nutritional Information per Serving: Calories: 304| Fat: 2.5g| Sat Fat: 0.9g| Carbohydrates: 16.2g| Fibre: 0.8g| Sugar: 1.2g| Protein: 5.2g

Mozzarella Cheese Bites

⏱ **Prep Time: 15 minutes**   🍲 **Cook: 8-10 minutes**   ≋ **Serves: 4**

Ingredients:

6 mozzarella string cheese sticks
30g all-purpose flour
2 large-sized eggs
110g panko breadcrumbs
1 teaspoon Italian herbs
1 teaspoon salt
Olive oil baking spray

Preparation:

1. Spray the inner basket of your Air Fryer with baking spray and slide it into the Air Fryer. 2. Set the Air Fryer at 175ºC to preheat for 4-5 minutes. 3. Cut each cheese stick into 4 even pieces. 4. Place the flour in a bowl. 5. Whisk the eggs and 2 teaspoons of water in a second bowl. 6. Put the breadcrumbs, Italian herbs, and salt into a third bowl and blend to incorporate. 7. Coat cheese cubes with flour, then dip into the egg mixture, and finally coat with breadcrumb mixture. 8. After preheating, place the cheese cubes in the preheated basket of Air Fryer and spray with baking spray. 9. Slide the basket inside and set the time for 8-10 minutes. 10. After the cooking period is finished, take off the cheese cubes from Air Fryer and enjoy moderately hot.

Nutritional Information per Serving: Calories: 289| Fat: 13.6g| Sat Fat: 6.9g| Carbohydrates: 28.3g| Fibre: 2.6g| Sugar: 2.3g| Protein: 17.2g

| Chapter 3 Snack & Appetizer Recipes

Parmesan Aubergines Chips

⏰ **Prep Time: 15 minutes** 🍱 **Cook: 5-10 minutes** ⚑ **Serves: 2**

Ingredients:

2 large eggs
1 medium aubergine (about 565g)
50g grated Parmesan cheese
1 teaspoon Italian seasoning
60g toasted wheat germ
¾ teaspoon garlic salt
Cooking spray

Preparation:

1. Mix the wheat germ, cheese, and all seasonings in a bowl. 2. In a separate bowl, whisk the egg. 3. Trim and cut aubergine lengthwise into ½-inch thick slices. 4. First, dip aubergine in eggs, then coat in the cheese mixture. 5. Grease the Air Fryer basket with cooking spray. 6. Set the Air Fryer at 200ºC to preheat for 4-5 minutes. 7. After preheating, place the aubergine in a single layer in the Air Fryer Basket. 8. Cook for around 5-10 minutes, shaking halfway through. 9. Once cooked, serve and enjoy.

Nutritional Information per Serving: Calories: 150| Fat: 8g| Sat Fat: 0.7g| Carbohydrates: 18g| Fibre: 12g| Sugar: 1g| Protein: 11g

Courgette Pizza Boats

⏰ **Prep Time: 5 minutes** 🍱 **Cook: 10 minutes** ⚑ **Serves: 4**

Ingredients:

2 courgettes
30g mozzarella cheese, shredded
120g pizza sauce

Preparation:

1. Set the Air Fryer at 175ºC to preheat for 4-5 minutes. 2. Start by cutting the courgette into halves, then take out the flesh. 3. Fill the courgette cavity with pizza sauce, then sprinkle some cheese over the top. 4. After preheating, place the courgette boats in the Air Fryer Basket. 5. Slide the basket inside and set the time for 10 minutes. 6. Once done, serve and enjoy.

Nutritional Information per Serving: Calories: 51| Fat: 3g| Sat Fat: 2g| Carbohydrates: 3g| Fibre: 1g| Sugar: 3g| Protein: 4g

Pasta Chips

⏰ **Prep Time: 10 minutes** 🍱 **Cook: 10 minutes** ⚑ **Serves: 2**

Ingredients:

1 teaspoon Italian Seasoning Blend
200g bow tie pasta, cooked and drained
1 tablespoon nutritional yeast
1 tablespoon aquafaba
Salt and black pepper, to taste

Preparation:

1. Set the Air Fryer at 200ºC to preheat for 4-5 minutes. 2. Toss the pasta with Italian seasoning, aquafaba, salt, yeast, and black pepper. 3. Add the mixtures to the baking pan. 4. After preheating, place the baking pan in the Air Fryer Basket. 5. Slide the basket inside and set the time for 5-10 minutes. 6. Shake the basket halfway through the cooking time. 7. Once cooked, serve and enjoy.

Nutritional Information per Serving: Calories: 230| Fat: 7g| Sat Fat: 0.8g| Carbohydrates: 34g| Fibre: 2g| Sugar: 0.5g| Protein: 9.6g

Chapter 4 Poultry Recipes

Chicken Milanese with Basil Tomato Sauce

⏲ **Prep Time: 15 minutes** 🍲 **Cook: 12 minutes** 🍽 **Serves: 4**

Ingredients:

For the Chicken:
45g Panko breadcrumbs
25g grated Parmesan cheese
4 boneless and skinless chicken breasts
Salt and powdered black pepper, as desired
Olive oil baking spray

For the Sauce:
2 teaspoons olive oil
1 shallot, cut up
300g grape tomatoes, halved
Salt and powdered black pepper, as desired
60ml red wine
10g fresh basil leaves, torn

Preparation:

1. Arrange each chicken breast between two pieces of plastic wrap and gently pound them into ½ inch thickness. 2. Rub each chicken breast with salt and pepper. 3. In a shallow dish, blend together the breadcrumbs and Parmesan cheese. 4. Spray each chicken breast lightly with baking spray. 5. Coat each chicken breast with breadcrumb mixture. 6. Spray the inner basket of your Air Fryer with baking spray and slide it into the Air Fryer. 7. Set the Air Fryer at 200ºC to preheat for 4-5 minutes. 8. After preheating, place the chicken breasts in the preheated basket of Air Fryer. 9. Slide the basket inside and set the time for 12 minutes. 10. While cooking, turn the chicken breasts once halfway through. 11. In the meantime, sizzle the oil into a wok on burner at medium heat. 12. Cook the shallot for around 2-3 minutes. 13. Put in tomatoes, salt, and pepper and blend. Cook for around 5 minutes. 14. Put in wine and blend. Cook for around 3-4 minutes. 15. Blend in basil and take off from burner. 16. After the cooking period is finished, take off the chicken breasts from Air Fryer and place onto serving plates. 17. Enjoy alongside the sauce.

Nutritional Information per Serving: Calories: 364| Fat: 21.6g| Sat Fat: 3g| Carbohydrates: 11g| Fibre: 2g| Sugar: 3g| Protein: 52g

Easy Pesto Chicken Breasts

⏲ **Prep Time: 10 minutes** 🍲 **Cook: 15-18 minutes** 🍽 **Serves: 4**

Ingredients:

4 (115g) chicken breasts
Salt and powdered black pepper, as desired
250g pesto
Olive oil baking spray

Preparation:

1. Spray the inner basket of your Air Fryer with baking spray and slide it into the Air Fryer. 2. Set the Air Fryer at 190ºC to preheat for 4-5 minutes. 3. Rub the chicken breasts with salt and pepper. 4. Coat the chicken breasts with pesto sauce. 5. After preheating, place the chicken breasts in the preheated basket of Air Fryer. 6. Slide the basket inside and set the time for 15-18 minutes. 7. While cooking, turn the chicken breasts once halfway through. 8. After the cooking period is finished, take off the chicken breasts from Air Fryer and enjoy right away.

Nutritional Information per Serving: Calories: 464| Fat: 41.1. 6g| Sat Fat: 10.1g| Carbohydrates: 9.3g| Fibre: 1.6g| Sugar: 2.3g| Protein: 53.2g

Lemon Chicken Thighs

⏰ **Prep Time: 10 minutes** 🍲 **Cook: 20 minutes** ❖ **Serves: 4**

Ingredients:

4 (170g) chicken thighs
2 tablespoons olive oil
2 tablespoons fresh lemon juice
1 tablespoon Italian seasoning
Salt and powdered black pepper, as desired
Olive oil baking spray

Preparation:

1. In a large-sized bowl, put the chicken thighs and remaining ingredients except for baking spray and blend to incorporate thoroughly. 2. Put the chicken thighs into your fridge to marinate for 30 minutes. 3. Take off the chicken thighs and let any excess marinade drip off. 4. Spray the inner basket of your Air Fryer with baking spray and slide it into the Air Fryer. 5. Set the Air Fryer at 175ºC to preheat for 4-5 minutes. 6. After preheating, place the chicken thighs in the preheated basket of Air Fryer. 7. Slide the basket inside and set the time for 20 minutes. 8. While cooking, turn the chicken thighs once halfway through. 9. After the cooking period is finished, take off the chicken thighs from Air Fryer and enjoy right away.

Nutritional Information per Serving: Calories: 372| Fat: 18g| Sat Fat: 4.3g| Carbohydrates: 0.6g| Fibre: 0.1g| Sugar: 0.4g| Protein: 49.3g

Crispy Crumbed Chicken Cutlets

⏰ **Prep Time: 15 minutes** 🍲 **Cook: 30 minutes** ❖ **Serves: 4**

Ingredients:

90g all-purpose flour
2 large-sized eggs
125g panko breadcrumbs
25g Parmesan cheese, grated
1 tablespoon mustard powder
Salt and powdered black pepper, as desired
4 (170g) boneless and skinless chicken cutlets
Olive oil baking spray
1 lemon, cut into slices

Preparation:

1. Spray the inner basket of your Air Fryer with baking spray and slide it into the Air Fryer. 2. Set the Air Fryer at 180ºC to preheat for 4-5 minutes. 3. In a shallow bowl, put the flour. 4. In a second bowl, crack the eggs and whisk well. 5. In a third bowl, blend together the breadcrumbs, cheese, mustard powder, salt, and black pepper. 6. Sprinkle the chicken with salt and black pepper. 7. Coat the chicken with flour, then dip into whisked eggs and finally coat with the breadcrumb mixture. 8. After preheating, place the chicken cutlets in the preheated basket of Air Fryer. 9. Slide the basket inside and set the time for 30 minutes. 10. While cooking, turn the chicken cutlets once halfway through. 11. After the cooking period is finished, take off the chicken cutlets from Air Fryer and enjoy right away with the topping of lemon slices.

Nutritional Information per Serving: Calories: 504| Fat: 41.6g| Sat Fat: 10.9g| Carbohydrates: 41.3g| Fibre: 9.6g| Sugar: 1.3g| Protein: 49.2g

Herbed Roasted Whole Chicken

⏱ **Prep Time: 15 minutes** 🍳 **Cook: 1 hour** 🍽 **Serves: 8**

Ingredients:

3 cloves garlic, minced
1 teaspoon fresh lemon zest, finely grated
1 teaspoon dried thyme, crushed
1 teaspoon dried oregano, crushed
1 teaspoon dried rosemary, crushed
Salt and powdered black pepper, as desired
2 tablespoons fresh lemon juice
2 tablespoons olive oil
1 (2265g) whole chicken

Preparation:

1. In a bowl, blend together the garlic, lemon zest, herbs, salt, and pepper. 2. Rub the chicken with herb mixture. 3. Drizzle the chicken with lemon juice and oil. 4. Set aside at the room temperature for around 2 hours. 5. Spray the inner basket of your Air Fryer with baking spray and slide it into the Air Fryer. 6. Set the Air Fryer at 180ºC to preheat for 4-5 minutes. 7. After preheating, place the chicken in the preheated basket of Air Fryer. 8. Slide the basket inside and set the time for 50 minutes. 9. While cooking, turn the chicken once halfway through. 10. After the cooking period is finished, take off the chicken from Air Fryer and place onto a chopping board for around 10 minutes. 11. Cut the chicken into serving portions and enjoy.

Nutritional Information per Serving: Calories: 860| Fat: 50g| Sat Fat: 15.9g| Carbohydrates: 1.3g| Fibre: 1.1g| Sugar: 0.2g| Protein: 71.1g

Mustard-Herb Chicken Drumsticks

⏱ **Prep Time: 10 minutes** 🍳 **Cook: 20 minutes** 🍽 **Serves: 4**

Ingredients:

60g Dijon mustard
1 tablespoon honey
2 tablespoons olive oil
½ tablespoon fresh rosemary, minced
1 tablespoon fresh thyme, minced
Salt and powdered black pepper, as desired
4 (170g) chicken drumsticks
Olive oil baking spray

Preparation:

1. In a bowl, blend together the mustard, honey, oil, herbs, salt, and black pepper. 2. Put in the drumsticks and coat with the mixture generously. 3. Cover the drumsticks and put into your fridge to marinate overnight. 4. Spray the inner basket of your Air Fryer with baking spray and slide it into the Air Fryer. 5. Set the Air Fryer at 160ºC to preheat for 4-5 minutes. 6. After preheating, place the chicken drumsticks in the preheated basket of Air Fryer. 7. Slide the basket inside and set the time for 10 minutes. 8. After 10 minutes of cooking, set the Air Fryer at 180ºC for 10 minutes. 9. After the cooking period is finished, take off the chicken drumsticks from Air Fryer and enjoy right away.

Nutritional Information per Serving: Calories: 377| Fat: 17.5g| Sat Fat: 3.7g| Carbohydrates: 5.9g| Fibre: 1g| Sugar: 4.5g| Protein: 47.6g

Sausage Stuffed Chicken Breast

⏰ **Prep Time: 10 minutes** 🍲 **Cook: 15 minutes** ❖ **Serves: 4**

Ingredients:

4 (115g) boneless and skinless chicken breasts
4 sausage links, casing removed
Olive oil baking spray

Preparation:

1. With a rolling pin, roll each chicken breast for around 1 minute. 2. Arrange the chicken breasts onto a smooth surface. 3. Place 1 sausage over each chicken breast. 4. Roll each breast around the sausage and secure with toothpicks. 5. Spray the inner basket of your Air Fryer with baking spray and slide it into the Air Fryer. 6. Set the Air Fryer at 190ºC to preheat for 4-5 minutes. 7. After preheating, place the chicken breasts in the preheated basket of Air Fryer. 8. Slide the basket inside and set the time for 15 minutes. 9. After the cooking period is finished, take off the chicken breasts from Air Fryer and enjoy right away.

Nutritional Information per Serving: Calories: 423| Fat: 27.6g| Sat Fat: 9.1g| Carbohydrates: 0g| Fibre: 0g| Sugar: 0g| Protein: 20.2g

Classic Chicken Parmigiana

⏰ **Prep Time: 10 minutes** 🍲 **Cook: 15 minutes** ❖ **Serves: 2**

Ingredients:

2 (170g) boneless and skinless chicken breasts
1 egg, whisked
115g breadcrumbs
1 tablespoon fresh basil
2 tablespoons olive oil
Olive oil baking spray
60g pasta sauce
25g Parmesan cheese, grated

Preparation:

1. Spray the inner basket of your Air Fryer with baking spray and slide it into the Air Fryer. 2. Set the Air Fryer at 175ºC to preheat for 4-5 minutes. 3. In a shallow bowl, whisk the egg. 4. In another bowl, put the oil, breadcrumbs, and basil and blend to form a crumbly mixture. 5. Now, dip each chicken breast into the whisked egg and then coat with the breadcrumb mixture. 6. After preheating, place the chicken breasts in the preheated basket of Air Fryer. 7. Slide the basket inside and set the time for 15 minutes. 8. After 12 minutes of cooking, spoon the pasta sauce over each chicken breast and sprinkle with cheese. 9. After the cooking period is finished, take off the chicken breasts from Air Fryer and enjoy right away.

Nutritional Information per Serving: Calories: 768| Fat: 35.4g| Sat Fat: 8.8g| Carbohydrates: 45.7g| Fibre: 3.4g| Sugar: 6.5g| Protein: 63.9g

Spinach Stuffed Chicken Breasts

⏰ **Prep Time: 15 minutes**   🍲 **Cook: 25 minutes**   🍽 **Serves: 2**

Ingredients:

1 tablespoon olive oil
50g fresh spinach
60g ricotta cheese, shredded
2 (115g) boneless and skinless chicken breasts
Salt and powdered black pepper, as desired
2 tablespoons Parmesan cheese, grated
¼ teaspoon paprika
Olive oil baking spray

Preparation:

1. In a medium-sized wok, sizzle the oil on burner at medium heat. 2. Cook the spinach for around 3-4 minutes. 3. Blend in the ricotta and cook for around 40-60 seconds. 4. Take off the wok from heat and set aside to cool. 5. Cut slits into the chicken breasts about ¼-inch apart but not all the way through. 6. Stuff each chicken breast with the spinach mixture. 7. Rub each chicken breast with salt and black pepper and then sprinkle with Parmesan cheese and paprika. 8. Spray the inner basket of your Air Fryer with baking spray and slide it into the Air Fryer. 9. Set the Air Fryer at 200ºC to preheat for 4-5 minutes. 10. After preheating, place the chicken breasts in the preheated basket of Air Fryer. 11. Slide the basket inside and set the time for 25 minutes. 12. After the cooking period is finished, take off the chicken breasts from Air Fryer and enjoy right away.

Nutritional Information per Serving: Calories: 269| Fat: 14.8g| Sat Fat: 4.7g| Carbohydrates: 2.6g| Fibre: 0.7g| Sugar: 0.2g| Protein: 31.6g

Chicken Spiedini

⏰ **Prep Time: 15 minutes**   🍲 **Cook: 12 minutes**   🍽 **Serves: 4**

Ingredients:

455g boneless and skinless chicken breasts
110g breadcrumbs
1 tablespoon olive oil
35g Parmesan cheese, grated
1 tablespoon fresh parsley, cut up
1 teaspoon garlic powder
2 large-sized eggs
Olive oil baking spray

Preparation:

1. With a meat mallet, pound each chicken breast. 2. Cut each chicken breast into 1-inch wide and 4-inch-long strips. 3. Roll each strip and place 3-4 rolled pieces of chicken onto a metal skewer. 4. In a microwave-safe bowl, put the breadcrumbs and oil and blend thoroughly. 5. Microwave for around 90 seconds, stirring after every 30 seconds. Set it aside to cool. 6. Put in Parmesan, parsley, and garlic powder and blend to incorporate. 7. In a shallow dish, whisk the eggs. 8. Dip each chicken skewer into egg and then coat with breadcrumb mixture. 9. Spray the inner basket of your Air Fryer with baking spray and slide it into the Air Fryer. 10. Set the Air Fryer at 190ºC to preheat for 4-5 minutes. 11. After preheating, place the skewers in the preheated basket of Air Fryer. 12. Slide the basket inside and set the time for 12 minutes. 13. While cooking, turn the skewers once halfway through. 14. After the cooking period is finished, take off the skewers from Air Fryer and enjoy right away.

Nutritional Information per Serving: Calories: 414| Fat: 34.6g| Sat Fat: 10.9g| Carbohydrates: 18.3g| Fibre: 1g| Sugar: 2g| Protein: 31.2g

Parmesan Chicken Meatballs

⏰ **Prep Time: 15 minutes**   🍳 **Cook: 10-12 minutes**   📚 **Serves: 6**

Ingredients:

455g ground chicken
25g breadcrumbs
25g Parmesan cheese, grated
1 large-sized egg
1 tablespoon fresh parsley, cut up
¼ teaspoon Italian seasoning
1 teaspoon garlic powder
Salt and powdered black pepper, as desired
Olive oil baking spray

Preparation:

1. Put the ground chicken and remaining ingredients except baking spray into a large-sized bowl and blend to incorporate. 2. Shape the chicken mixture into 1-inch meatballs. 3. Spray the inner basket of your Air Fryer with baking spray and slide it into the Air Fryer. 4. Set the Air Fryer at 190ºC to preheat for 4-5 minutes. 5. After preheating, place the meatballs in the preheated basket of Air Fryer. 6. Slide the basket inside and set the time for 10-12 minutes. 7. While cooking, turn the meatballs once halfway through. 8. After the cooking period is finished, take off the meatballs from Air Fryer and enjoy right away.

Nutritional Information per Serving: Calories: 156| Fat: 8g| Sat Fat: 3g| Carbohydrates: 4.3g| Fibre: 0.3g| Sugar: 0.4g| Protein: 16.2g

Herbed Roasted Turkey Breast

⏰ **Prep Time: 10 minutes**   🍳 **Cook: 1 hour**   📚 **Serves: 8**

Ingredients:

2 tablespoons olive oil
2 tablespoons lemon juice
1 tablespoon garlic, minced
2 teaspoons powdered mustard
Salt and powdered black pepper, as desired
1 teaspoon powdered sage
1 teaspoon dried thyme
1 teaspoon dried rosemary
1 (1369g) turkey breast
Olive oil baking spray

Preparation:

1. Spray the inner basket of your Air Fryer with baking spray and slide it into the Air Fryer. 2. Set the Air Fryer at 180ºC to preheat for 4-5 minutes. 3. In a small-sized bowl, put the oil and remaining ingredients except the turkey breast and baking spray, and blend to incorporate thoroughly. 4. Rub the oil mixture on the outside of the turkey breast and under any loose skin generously. 5. After preheating, place the turkey breast in the preheated basket of Air Fryer, skin side up. 6. Slide the basket inside and set the time for 60 minutes. 7. After the cooking period is finished, take off the turkey breast from Air Fryer and place onto a platter for around 5-10 minutes. 8. Cut the turkey breast into serving portions and enjoy.

Nutritional Information per Serving: Calories: 214| Fat: 6.6g| Sat Fat: 1.1g| Carbohydrates: 8.1g| Fibre: 1.2g| Sugar: 6.1g| Protein: 29.4g

Homemade Turkey Burgers

⏱ **Prep Time: 10 minutes** 🍳 **Cook: 15 minutes** 🍽 **Serves: 2**

Ingredients:

230g ground turkey
30g feta cheese, crumbled
1½ tablespoons extra-virgin olive oil
2 cloves garlic, grated
2 teaspoons fresh oregano, cut up
½ teaspoon red pepper flakes, crushed
Salt, as desired
Olive oil baking spray

Preparation:

1. Spray the inner basket of your Air Fryer with baking spray and slide it into the Air Fryer. 2. Set the Air Fryer at 175ºC to preheat for 4-5 minutes. 3. In a large-sized bowl, put the ground turkey and remaining ingredients except baking spray and blend to incorporate thoroughly. 4. Make 2 (½-inch-thick) patties from the mixture. 5. After preheating, place the patties in the preheated basket of Air Fryer. 6. Slide the basket inside and set the time for 15 minutes. 7. While cooking, turn the patties once halfway through. 8. After the cooking period is finished, take off the patties from Air Fryer and enjoy right away.

Nutritional Information per Serving: Calories: 364| Fat: 23.1g| Sat Fat: 6.7g| Carbohydrates: 3g| Fibre: 0.8g| Sugar: 0.9g| Protein: 35.6g

Turkey Pepperoni Calzones

⏱ **Prep Time: 20 minutes** 🍳 **Cook: 10 minutes** 🍽 **Serves: 2**

Ingredients:

225g pizza dough
60g pizza sauce
60g mozzarella cheese, shredded
55g turkey pepperoni
Olive oil baking spray

Preparation:

1. Divide the pizza dough into 2 equal-sized pieces. 2. With your hands, roll out each dough piece into a pizza shape. 3. Spread the pizza sauce on half of each dough circle, leaving the edges. 4. Top the sauce with a layer of cheese, followed by pepperoni and another layer of cheese. 5. Fold over the other side of dough to create a half-circle shape. 6. With your fingers, crimp the edges to seal the filling. 7. Spray the inner basket of your Air Fryer with baking spray and slide it into the Air Fryer. 8. Set the Air Fryer at 190ºC to preheat for 4-5 minutes. 9. After preheating, place the calzones in the preheated basket of Air Fryer. 10. Slide the basket inside and set the time for 10 minutes. 11. While cooking, turn the calzones once halfway through. 12. After the cooking period is finished, take off the calzones from Air Fryer and enjoy moderately hot.

Nutritional Information per Serving: Calories: 590| Fat: 29.6g| Sat Fat: 12g| Carbohydrates: 57g| Fibre: 2g| Sugar: 9g| Protein: 28g

Chicken Parmesan Meatballs with Pasta

⏰ **Prep Time: 20 minutes**   🍲 **Cook: 16 minutes**   ⬗ **Serves: 2**

Ingredients:

1 egg
635g ground chicken breast
215g cooked pasta
110g breadcrumbs
40g shredded mozzarella cheese
1 tablespoon Italian seasoning
50g parmesan cheese
Salt and black pepper, to taste
125g marinara sauce

Preparation:

1. Set the Air Fryer at 190ºC to preheat for 4-5 minutes. 2. In a large mixing bowl, mix the parmesan cheese, black pepper, salt, eggs, breadcrumbs, and Italian seasoning. 3. Add the chicken and mix well, then form meatballs. 4. Coat the meatballs with oil spray. 5. Grease the baking pan with oil spray and place the chicken meatballs in the pan. 6. After preheating, add the baking pan to the Air Fryer basket. 7. Slide the basket inside and set the time for 12 minutes, flipping halfway through. 8. Pour the marinara sauce on top of each chicken meatball and top with the mozzarella cheese. Cook for 4 more minutes. 9. Serve over the pasta, and enjoy.

Nutritional Information per Serving: Calories: 633| Fat: 20g| Sat Fat: 5g| Carbohydrates: 81g| Fibre: 7g| Sugar: 13g| Protein: 33g
60.

Parmesan Chicken Tenders

⏰ **Prep Time: 10 minutes**   🍲 **Cook: 15 minutes**   ⬗ **Serves: 2**

Ingredients:

455g skinless chicken breast, cut into strips
55g Panko bread crumbs
100g parmesan cheese, grated
2 eggs
¼ teaspoon paprika
120ml buttermilk
Salt and black pepper, to taste
Oil spray, for greasing

Preparation:

1. Set the Air Fryer at 200ºC to preheat for 4-5 minutes. 2. Whisk the eggs with buttermilk in a bowl. 3. Combine together the Panko bread crumbs, salt, parmesan cheese, pepper, and paprika in a separate bowl. 4. Dip the chicken strips in the egg wash, then coat inside the parmesan cheese mix. 5. Coat the chicken from all sides with oil spray. 6. After preheating, place the chicken strips in the Air Fryer Basket. 7. Slide the basket inside and set the time for 15 minutes, flipping halfway through. 8. Once finished, serve and enjoy.

Nutritional Information per Serving: Calories: 230| Fat: 10g| Sat Fat: 2g| Carbohydrates: 15g| Fibre: 1.3g| Sugar: 2g| Protein: 19g

Chicken Parmesan

⏰ **Prep Time: 15 minutes** 🍲 **Cook: 13 minutes** ❖ **Serves: 4**

Ingredients:

4 (115g) boneless and skinless chicken breasts, pounded
Salt and powdered black pepper, as desired
40g all-purpose flour
2 large eggs
160g panko breadcrumbs
25g Parmesan cheese, finely grated
1 teaspoon dried oregano
½ teaspoon red pepper flakes
½ teaspoon garlic powder
250g marinara sauce
115g mozzarella cheese, shredded
Olive oil baking spray
1 tablespoon parsley fresh, finely cut up

Preparation:

1. Sprinkle the chicken fillets with salt and pepper. 2. Put the flour, salt, and pepper into a shallow dish and blend. 3. Whisk the eggs into a second shallow dish. 4. Put the panko, Parmesan, oregano, red pepper flakes, and garlic powder into a third shallow dish and blend. 5. Coat each chicken piece with flour, then dip into eggs, and finally coat with panko mixture. 6. Spray the inner basket of your Air Fryer with baking spray and then slide it in the Air Fryer. 7. Set the Air Fryer at 200ºC to preheat for 4-5 minutes. 8. After preheating, place the chicken pieces in the preheated basket of Air Fryer. 9. Slide the basket back into the Air Fryer and set the time for 13 minutes. 10. After 5 minutes of cooking, flip the chicken pieces. 11. After 10 minutes of cooking, top each chicken piece with marinara, followed by mozzarella cheese. 12. After the cooking period is finished, take off the chicken pieces from Air Fryer and enjoy right away with the garnishing of parsley.

Nutritional Information per Serving: Calories: 583| Fat: 18.4g| Sat Fat: 4.1g| Carbohydrates: 45.7g| Fibre: 3.4g| Sugar: 6.1g| Protein: 57.9g

Chicken Margherita

⏰ **Prep Time: 20 minutes** 🍲 **Cook: 25 minutes** ❖ **Serves: 4**

Ingredients:

110g cherry tomatoes, halved
2 tablespoons fresh basil leaves, sliced
1 tablespoon fresh lemon Juice
2 (170g) skinless & boneless chicken breasts, pounded slightly
1 tablespoon olive oil
Salt and ground black pepper, as desired
65g pesto
Olive oil baking spray
2 mozzarella cheese slices

Preparation:

1. Put the tomatoes, basil, and lemon juice into a medium-size bowl and toss to incorporate. 2. Put the chicken breasts, oil, salt, and pepper into a zip lock bag. 3. Seal the bag and shake to coat thoroughly. 4. Spray the inner basket of your Air Fryer with baking spray and then slide it in the Air Fryer. 5. Set the Air Fryer at 200ºC to preheat for 4-5 minutes. 6. After preheating, place the chicken breasts in the preheated basket of Air Fryer. 7. Slide the basket back into the Air Fryer and set the time for 25 minutes. 8. After 10 minutes of cooking, flip the chicken breasts. 9. After 20 minutes of cooking, top each chicken breast with pesto, followed by mozzarella slice and tomato mixture. 10. After the cooking period is finished, take off the chicken breasts from Air Fryer and enjoy right away.

Nutritional Information per Serving: Calories: 395| Fat: 27.4g| Sat Fat: 8.1g| Carbohydrates: 7.7g| Fibre: 1g| Sugar: 3.1g| Protein: 32.9g

Italian Marinated Chicken Thighs

⏰ **Prep Time: 10 minutes** 🍲 **Cook: 30 minutes** ≋ **Serves: 4**

Ingredients:

4 (170-gram) bone-in & skin-on chicken thighs
Salt and ground black pepper, as desired
230g Italian salad dressing
1 teaspoon onion powder
1 teaspoon garlic powder
Olive oil baking spray

Preparation:

1. Sprinkle the chicken thighs with salt and pepper.2. Put the chicken thighs and dressing into a large-sized bowl and blend to incorporate.3. Cover the bowl and put into your fridge to marinate overnight.4. Take off the chicken breast from the bowl and place onto a plate.5. Sprinkle the chicken thighs with onion powder and garlic powder.6. Spray the inner basket of your Air Fryer with baking spray and then slide it in the Air Fryer.7. Set the Air Fryer at 180ºC to preheat for 4-5 minutes.8. After preheating, place the chicken thighs in the preheated basket of Air Fryer.9. Slide the basket back into the Air Fryer and set the time for 30 minutes.10. While cooking, turn the chicken thighs once halfway through.11. After the cooking period is finished, take off the chicken thighs from Air Fryer and enjoy right away.

Nutritional Information per Serving: Calories: 414| Fat: 21.4g| Sat Fat: 8.8g| Carbohydrates: 1.1g| Fibre: 0.1g| Sugar: 1.5g| Protein: 48.9g

Italian Stuffed Chicken Breasts

⏰ **Prep Time: 15 minutes** 🍲 **Cook: 25 minutes** ≋ **Serves: 4**

Ingredients:

200g Italian cheese blend, shredded and divided
1 clove garlic, finely cut up
2 tablespoons fresh basil, cut up
2 tablespoons fresh oregano, cut up
4 (115g) boneless and skinless chicken breasts
1 egg
50g Parmesan cheese, grated
70g Italian-seasoned breadcrumbs
Olive oil baking spray
250g spaghetti sauce

Preparation:

1. Put the 170g of Italian cheese blend, garlic, basil, and oregano into a bowl and blend. 2. Cut a slit into the chicken breast about ¼-inch apart but not all the way through.3. Lightly pound chicken to flatten.4. Stuff each chicken breast with the Italian cheese mixture.5. Whisk the egg into a shallow dish.6. Put the Parmesan cheese and breadcrumbs into a separate shallow dish and blend.7. Dip each chicken breast into egg and then coat with breadcrumb mixture.8. Spray the inner basket of your Air Fryer with baking spray and then slide it in the Air Fryer.9. Set the Air Fryer at 160ºC to preheat for 4-5 minutes.10. After preheating, place the chicken breasts in the preheated basket of Air Fryer.11. Slide the basket back into the Air Fryer and set the time for 25 minutes.12. After 20 minutes of cooking, top each chicken breast with spaghetti sauce, followed by remaking Italian cheese. 13. After the cooking period is finished, take off the chicken breasts from Air Fryer and enjoy right away.

Nutritional Information per Serving: Calories: 471| Fat: 23.4g| Sat Fat: 11.8g| Carbohydrates: 22.7g| Fibre: 3.1g| Sugar: 6.5g| Protein: 43.9g

Classic Chicken Piccata

⏱ **Prep Time: 15 minutes**   🍲 **Cook: 14 minutes**   ❖ **Serves: 4**

Ingredients:

2 large eggs
3 tablespoons lemon juice, divided
1 teaspoon garlic powder
60g all-purpose flour
50g Parmesan cheese, grated
2 tablespoons dried parsley flakes
Salt, as desired
4 (115g) boneless and skinless chicken breasts, pounded
Olive oil baking spray
2 tablespoons butter
60ml chicken broth
2 tablespoons capers with liquid

Preparation:

1. Put the eggs, 1 tablespoon of lemon juice, and garlic powder into a shallow dish and whisk to incorporate thoroughly. 2. Put the flour, Parmesan, parsley, and salt into another shallow dish and blend to incorporate thoroughly.3. Coat the chicken pieces with flour mixture, then dip into egg mixture, and again, coat with flour mixture.4. Spray the inner basket of your Air Fryer with baking spray and then slide it in the Air Fryer.5. Set the Air Fryer at 190ºC to preheat for 4-5 minutes.6. After preheating, place the chicken pieces in the preheated basket of Air Fryer.7. Slide the basket back into the Air Fryer and set the time for 14 minutes.8. In the meantime, sizzle the butter into a small-sized pot on burner at medium heat.9. Put in the broth, remaining lemon juice, and capers with their liquid and cook until boiling.10. Turn the heat at around medium-low. Cook for around 2-3 minutes.11. After the cooking period is finished, take off the chicken pieces from Air Fryer and transfer to serving plates.12. Drizzle with the lemon sauce and enjoy right away.

Nutritional Information per Serving: Calories: 323| Fat: 14.4g| Sat Fat: 6.8g| Carbohydrates: 15.7g| Fibre: 1.3g| Sugar: 1g| Protein: 33.7g

Chapter 5 Red Meat Recipes

Herbed Beef Roast

⏰ **Prep Time: 10 minutes**   🍲 **Cook: 45 minutes**   ⚜ **Serves: 6**

Ingredients:

910g beef roast
1 tablespoon olive oil
1 teaspoon dried rosemary, crushed
1 teaspoon dried thyme, crushed
1 teaspoon dried parsley, crushed
Salt, as desired
Olive oil baking spray

Preparation:

1. Spray the inner basket of your Air Fryer with baking spray and slide it into the Air Fryer. 2. Set the Air Fryer at 180ºC to preheat for 4-5 minutes. 3. In a bowl, blend together the oil, herbs, and salt. 4. Coat the roast with herb mixture. 5. After preheating, place the roast in the preheated basket of Air Fryer. 6. Slide the basket inside and set the time for 45 minutes. 7. After the cooking period is finished, take off the roast from Air Fryer and place onto a platter. 8. With a piece of foil, cover the roast for around 10 minutes. 9. Cut the roast into serving portions and enjoy.

Nutritional Information per Serving: Calories: 304| Fat: 11.8g| Sat Fat: 3.9g| Carbohydrates: 0.3g| Fibre: 0.2g| Sugar: 0g| Protein: 45.9g

Lemony Garlic Flank Steak

⏰ **Prep Time: 10 minutes**   🍲 **Cook: 15 minutes**   ⚜ **Serves: 6**

Ingredients:

910g flank steak
3 tablespoons fresh lemon juice
2 tablespoons olive oil
3 cloves garlic, minced
1 teaspoon Italian seasoning
Salt and powdered black pepper, as desired
Olive oil baking spray

Preparation:

1. In a large-sized bowl, put the steak and remaining ingredients except baking spray and blend to incorporate. 2. Put into your fridge to marinate for 24 hours, flipping occasionally. 3. Spray the inner basket of your Air Fryer with baking spray and slide it into the Air Fryer. 4. Set the Air Fryer at 200ºC to preheat for 4-5 minutes. 5. After preheating, place the steak in the preheated basket of Air Fryer. 6. Slide the basket inside and set the time for 15 minutes. 7. While cooking, turn the steak once halfway through. 8. After the cooking period is finished, take off the steak from Air Fryer and place onto a platter. 9. Cut the steak into serving portions and enjoy.

Nutritional Information per Serving: Calories: 339| Fat: 17.4g| Sat Fat: 6g| Carbohydrates: 0.9g| Fibre: 0.2g| Sugar: 0.2g| Protein: 42.3g

Crispy Beef Stromboli

⏰ **Prep Time: 20 minutes** 🍲 **Cook: 30 minutes** ≋ **Serves: 4**

Ingredients:

225g rib-eye steak, shaved
115g onions, cut up
220g green bell pepper, cut up
2 teaspoons garlic, minced
2 tablespoons Worcestershire Sauce
1 tablespoon fresh lime juice
1 teaspoon sea salt
½ teaspoon black pepper
12 provolone cheese slices
1 frozen puff pastry sheet, thawed
1 large-sized egg, whisked
½ tablespoons steak seasoning

Preparation:

1. Slide the inner basket of your Air Fryer into the Air Fryer and set at 200ºC to preheat for 4-5 minutes. 2. In a large-sized mixing, put the steak, onions, bell pepper, garlic, Worcestershire Sauce, lime juice, salt, and pepper and blend to incorporate. 3. Place the steak mixture into a baking pan. 4. After preheating, place the baking pan in the Air Fryer Basket. 5. Slide the basket inside and set the time for 15 minutes. 6. After the cooking period is finished, take off the baking pan from Air Fryer and set aside to cool for around 10-15 minutes. 7. Arrange the puff pastry sheet onto a lightly floured surface and roll out it. 8. Spread the steak mixture over the top ¾ of puff pastry. 9. Top with provolone cheese slices. 10. Roll the puff pastry tightly towards the empty end. 11. Brush the puff pastry with whisked egg and then sprinkle with steak seasoning. 12. With a knife, make slits across the top of pastry. 13. Spray the inner basket of your Air Fryer with baking spray and slide it into the Air Fryer. 14. Set the Air Fryer at 190ºC to preheat for 4-5 minutes. 15. After preheating, place the stromboli in the preheated basket of Air Fryer. 16. Slide the basket inside and set the time for 15 minutes. 17. After 10 minutes of cooking, turn the stromboli. 18. After the cooking period is finished, take off the stromboli from Air Fryer and enjoy.

Nutritional Information per Serving: Calories: 359| Fat: 24g| Sat Fat: 10g| Carbohydrates: 20g| Fibre: 2g| Sugar: 3g| Protein: 17g

Garlic Steak Bites

⏰ **Prep Time: 10 minutes** 🍲 **Cook: 10 minutes** ≋ **Serves: 4**

Ingredients:

455g sirloin steak, cut into 1-inch cubes
3 cloves garlic, minced
3 tablespoons olive oil
1½ teaspoons Italian seasoning
1 teaspoon paprika
Salt and powdered black pepper, as desired
Olive oil baking spray

Preparation:

1. In a bowl, put the steak and remaining ingredients except baking spray and blend to incorporate thoroughly. 2. Set it aside for around 15-20 minutes. 3. Spray the inner basket of your Air Fryer with baking spray and slide it into the Air Fryer. 4. Set the Air Fryer at 200ºC to preheat for 4-5 minutes. 5. After preheating, place the steak bites in the preheated basket of Air Fryer. 6. Slide the basket inside and set the time for 8-10 minutes. 7. After the cooking period is finished, take off the steak bites from Air Fryer and enjoy right away.

Nutritional Information per Serving: Calories: 293| Fat: 22g| Sat Fat: 7g| Carbohydrates: 2g| Fibre: 1g| Sugar: 0.1g| Protein: 25g

Ground Beef Stuffed Bell Peppers

⏰ **Prep Time:** 15 minutes 🍲 **Cook:** 15 minutes 🍃 **Serves:** 6

Ingredients:

6 bell peppers
565g lean ground beef
250g marinara sauce
30g scallion, cut up
15g fresh parsley, cut up
½ teaspoon dried sage, crushed
½ teaspoon garlic salt
1 tablespoon olive oil
30g mozzarella cheese, shredded
Olive oil baking spray

Preparation:

1. Cut the top off of each bell pepper and carefully take off the seeds. Set aside. 2. Heat a nonstick wok over medium-high heat and cook the beef for around 8-10 minutes. 3. Drain the fat thoroughly. 4. Put in the marinara sauce, scallion, parsley, sage, salt, and oil and blend to incorporate. 5. Stuff each bell pepper with beef mixture. 6. Spray the inner basket of your Air Fryer with baking spray and slide it into the Air Fryer. 7. Set the Air Fryer at 180ºC to preheat for 4-5 minutes. 8. After preheating, place the bell peppers in the preheated basket of Air Fryer. 9. Slide the basket inside and set the time for 15 minutes. 10. After 10 minutes of cooking, top each bell pepper with cheese. 11. After the cooking period is finished, take off the bell peppers from Air Fryer and enjoy right away.

Nutritional Information per Serving: Calories: 293| Fat: 18.2g| Sat Fat: 0.8g| Carbohydrates: 15.6g| Fibre: 2.9g| Sugar: 9.9g| Protein: 18.6g

Ground Beef Foil Packets with Vegetables

⏰ **Prep Time:** 10 minutes 🍲 **Cook:** 25 minutes 🍃 **Serves:** 4

Ingredients:

455g ground beef
225g green beans, trimmed
250g corn kernels
2 teaspoons onion powder
125g onion, chopped
2 teaspoons dried thyme
455g red potatoes, cut into 1-inch pieces
1 tablespoon garlic powder
1½ teaspoons kosher salt

Preparation:

1. Set the Air Fryer at 190ºC to preheat for 4-5 minutes. 2. Arrange four pieces of aluminium foil on your kitchen surface, and divide the potatoes, green beans, and onion equally between each packet. 3. Shape the foil around the potatoes, make four balls out of the ground beef, and add to each packet. 4. Whisk the thyme, garlic powder, salt, and onion powder in a small bowl and sprinkle the spice mixture on top of the ground beef foil packets. 5. After preheating, place the ground beef packet in the Air Fryer Basket. 6. Cook the beef foil packets for 25 minutes. 7. Serve and enjoy.

Nutritional Information per Serving: Calories: 374| Fat: 9g| Sat Fat: 4g| Carbohydrates: 36g| Fibre: 6g| Sugar: 0.7g| Protein: 27g

Pistachio-Crusted Rack of Lamb

⏱ **Prep Time: 15 minutes** 🍲 **Cook: 19 minutes** ❖ **Serves: 4**

Ingredients:

1 (680g) rack of lamb, trimmed all fat and frenched
Salt and powdered black pepper, as desired
Olive oil baking spray
35g pistachios, finely cut up
2 tablespoons panko breadcrumbs
2 teaspoons fresh thyme, finely cut up
1 teaspoon fresh rosemary, finely cut up
1 tablespoon butter, melted
1 tablespoon Dijon mustard

Preparation:

1. Spray the inner basket of your Air Fryer with baking spray and slide it into the Air Fryer. 2. Set the Air Fryer at 195ºC to preheat for 4-5 minutes. 3. Sprinkle the rack with salt and black pepper. 4. After preheating, place the rack of lamb in the preheated basket of Air Fryer. 5. Slide the basket inside and set the time for 12 minutes. 6. In the meantime, in a small-sized bowl, blend together the remaining ingredients except the mustard. 7. After the cooking period is finished, take off the rack of lamb from Air Fryer and brush the meaty side with mustard. 8. Then, coat the pistachio mixture on all sides of the rack and press firmly. 9. Again, set the Air Fryer at 195ºC. 10. Place the rack of lamb into the basket of Air Fryer, meat side up. 11. Slide the basket inside and set the time for 7 minutes. 12. After the cooking period is finished, take off the rack of lamb from Air Fryer and place onto a chopping board for at least 10 minutes. 13. Cut the rack into individual chops and enjoy.

Nutritional Information per Serving: Calories: 824| Fat: 39.3g| Sat Fat: 14.2g| Carbohydrates: 10.3 g| Fibre: 1.2g| Sugar: 0.2g| Protein: 72g

Pesto Rack of Lamb

⏱ **Prep Time: 15 minutes** 🍲 **Cook: 15 minutes** ❖ **Serves: 4**

Ingredients:

1 (680g) rack of lamb
Olive oil baking spray
For the Pesto:
½ bunch fresh mint
1 clove garlic
60ml extra-virgin olive oil
½ tablespoons honey
Salt and powdered black pepper, as desired

Preparation:

1. Spray the inner basket of your Air Fryer with baking spray and slide it into the Air Fryer. 2. Set the Air Fryer at 200ºC to preheat for 4-5 minutes. 3. For the pesto: in an electric blender, put the mint, garlic, oil, honey, salt, and black pepper and process to form a smooth mixture. 4. Coat the rack of lamb with pesto. 5. After preheating, place the rack of lamb in the preheated basket of Air Fryer. 6. Slide the basket inside and set the time for 15 minutes. 7. While cooking, coat the rack of lamb with the remaining pesto after every 5 minutes. 8. After the cooking period is finished, take off the rack of lamb from Air Fryer and place onto a chopping board for around 5 minutes. 9. Cut the rack into individual chops and enjoy.

Nutritional Information per Serving: Calories: 405| Fat: 27.7g| Sat Fat: 7.1g| Carbohydrates: 2.8g| Fibre: 0.3g| Sugar: 2.2g| Protein: 34.8g

Herbed Lamb Chops

⏱ **Prep Time: 10 minutes**   🍳 **Cook: 8-10 minutes**   ❖ **Serves: 2**

Ingredients:

1 tablespoon fresh lemon juice
1 tablespoon olive oil
1 teaspoon dried rosemary
1 teaspoon dried thyme
1 teaspoon dried oregano
½ teaspoon powdered cumin
Salt and powdered black pepper, as desired
4 (115g) lamb chops
Olive oil baking spray

Preparation:

1. In a large-sized bowl, blend together the lemon juice, oil, herbs, and spices. 2. Put in the chops and coat with the herb mixture. 3. Put into your fridge to marinate for around 1 hour. 4. Spray the inner basket of your Air Fryer with baking spray and slide it into the Air Fryer. 5. Set the Air Fryer at 200ºC to preheat for 4-5 minutes. 6. After preheating, place the chops in the preheated basket of Air Fryer. 7. Slide the basket inside and set the time for 8-10 minutes. 8. While cooking, turn the chops once halfway through. 9. After the cooking period is finished, take off the chops from Air Fryer and enjoy right away.

Nutritional Information per Serving: Calories: 491| Fat: 24g| Sat Fat: 7.1g| Carbohydrates: 1.6g| Fibre: 0.9g| Sugar: 0.2g| Protein: 64g

Lemony Garlic Lamb Chops

⏱ **Prep Time: 10 minutes**   🍳 **Cook: 10 minutes**   ❖ **Serves: 4**

Ingredients:

4 cloves garlic, crushed
1 tablespoon fresh lemon juice
1 teaspoon olive oil
1 tablespoon Italian seasoning
Kosher salt and powdered black pepper, as desired
8 (100g) bone-in lamb chops
Olive oil baking spray

Preparation:

1. Spray the inner basket of your Air Fryer with baking spray and slide it into the Air Fryer. 2. Set the Air Fryer at 200ºC to preheat for 4-5 minutes. 3. In a large-sized bowl, blend together the garlic, lemon juice, oil, Italian seasoning, salt, and black pepper. 4. Coat the chops with the garlic mixture. 5. After preheating, place the chops in the preheated basket of Air Fryer. 6. Slide the basket inside and set the time for 10 minutes. 7. While cooking, turn the chops once halfway through. 8. After the cooking period is finished, take off the chops from Air Fryer and enjoy right away.

Nutritional Information per Serving: Calories: 384| Fat: 15.6g| Sat Fat: 4.9g| Carbohydrates: 1g| Fibre: 0.1g| Sugar: 0.1g| Protein: 54.2g

Lamb Steak and Pasta

⏰ **Prep Time: 20 minutes** 🍲 **Cook: 30 minutes** ❖ **Serves: 4**

Ingredients:

170g baby spinach, chopped
120g feta cheese, crumbled
60g pesto
2 lamb steaks
60g walnuts, chopped
150g grape tomatoes, halved
Salt and black pepper, to taste
95g penne pasta, uncooked

Preparation:

1. Set the Air Fryer at 200ºC to preheat for 4-5 minutes. 2. Cook the pasta following the package instructions. 3. Once cooked, drain and set aside. 4. Season the lamb with pepper, salt, and oil. 5. After preheating, place the lamb in the Air Fryer Basket. Cook for around 12 minutes, flipping halfway through 6. In the meantime, add the cooked pasta, walnuts, tomatoes, spinach, and pesto sauce in a bowl. 7. When cooking is finished, place the cooked steak slices on the bowl and serve with feta crumbs.

Nutritional Information per Serving: Calories: 470| Fat: 14g| Sat Fat: 6g| Carbohydrates: 43g| Fibre: 2g| Sugar: 0.2g| Protein: 30g

Herbed Pork Chops

⏰ **Prep Time: 10 minutes** 🍲 **Cook: 12 minutes** ❖ **Serves: 2**

Ingredients:

2 cloves garlic, minced
½ tablespoon fresh coriander, cut up
½ tablespoon fresh rosemary, cut up
½ tablespoon fresh parsley, cut up
2 tablespoons olive oil
¾ tablespoon Dijon mustard
1 teaspoon sugar
Salt, as desired
2 (170g) pork chops
Olive oil baking spray

Preparation:

1. In a bowl, blend together the garlic, herbs, oil, mustard, coriander, sugar, and salt. 2. Put in the pork chops and generously coat with the herb mixture. 3. Cover and put into your fridge for around 2-3 hours. 4. Take off the chops from the refrigerator and set aside at room temperature for around 30 minutes. 5. Spray the inner basket of your Air Fryer with baking spray and slide it into the Air Fryer. 6. Set the Air Fryer at 200ºC to preheat for 4-5 minutes. 7. After preheating, place the chops in the preheated basket of Air Fryer. 8. Slide the basket inside and set the time for 12 minutes. 9. While cooking, turn the chops once halfway through. 10. After the cooking period is finished, take off the chops from Air Fryer and enjoy right away.

Nutritional Information per Serving: Calories: 504| Fat: 44.6g| Sat Fat: 15.6g| Carbohydrates: 3.9g| Fibre: 0.6g| Sugar: 2.1g| Protein: 30.2g

Rosemary Pork Loin

⏰ **Prep Time: 10 minutes** 🍲 **Cook: 20 minutes** 📚 **Serves: 6**

Ingredients:

3 tablespoons sugar
2 teaspoons dried rosemary
1 teaspoon garlic powder
Salt, as desired
910g pork loin
Olive oil baking spray

Preparation:

1. Spray the inner basket of your Air Fryer with baking spray and slide it into the Air Fryer. 2. Set the Air Fryer at 200ºC to preheat for 4-5 minutes. 3. In a bowl, put the sugar, basil, garlic powder, and salt and blend to incorporate. 4. Rub the pork loin with basil mixture generously. 5. After preheating, place the pork loin in the preheated basket of Air Fryer. 6. Slide the basket inside and set the time for 20 minutes. 7. While cooking, turn the pork loin once halfway through. 8. After the cooking period is finished, take off the pork loin from Air Fryer and place onto a chopping board. 9. Cut into serving portions and enjoy.

Nutritional Information per Serving: Calories: 391| Fat: 21.2g| Sat Fat: 7.9g| Carbohydrates: 6.3g| Fibre: 0.1g| Sugar: 5.3g| Protein: 41.2g

Ham and Pepperoni Sliders

⏰ **Prep Time: 15 minutes** 🍲 **Cook: 10-12 minutes** 📚 **Serves: 6**

Ingredients:

6 sweet rolls
60g mozzarella cheese, shredded
125g provolone cheese, shredded
6 slices salami slices
6 pepperoni slices
3 ham slices, halved
For the Garlic Butter:
2 tablespoons salted butter
2 tablespoons fresh parsley, minced
2 cloves garlic, minced
⅛ teaspoon salt
¼ teaspoon black pepper
¼ teaspoon Italian seasoning
¼ teaspoon red pepper flakes

Preparation:

1. Cut each roll in half. 2. Place the bottom half of each roll onto a platter. 3. Place a layer of both cheeses over each bun half and top with meat slices. 4. Top with another layer of both cheeses. 5. Cover with top halves of buns. 6. For the garlic butter: in a small-sized pot, sizzle butter on burner at low heat. 7. Cook the parsley and remaining ingredients for around 2 minutes. 8. Take off from burner. 9. Brush the sliders with garlic butter. 10. Spray the inner basket of your Air Fryer with baking spray and slide it into the Air Fryer. 11. Set the Air Fryer at 160ºC to preheat for 4-5 minutes. 12. After preheating, place the sliders in the preheated basket of Air Fryer. 13. Slide the basket inside and set the time for 8-10 minutes. 14. After the cooking period is finished, take off the sliders from Air Fryer and enjoy right away.

Nutritional Information per Serving: Calories: 348| Fat: 21.6g| Sat Fat: 12.9g| Carbohydrates: 12.8g| Fibre: 2.4g| Sugar: 7.3g| Protein: 29.2g

Chapter 5 Red Meat Recipes

Pork Meatballs

⏰ Prep Time: 15 minutes   🍲 Cook: 12 minutes   ⬥ Serves: 4

Ingredients:

455g ground pork
½ of medium-sized onion, roughly cut up
2 tablespoons fresh parsley, roughly cut up
2 cloves garlic, peeled
30g feta cheese, crumbled
35g Italian seasoned breadcrumbs
1 egg, lightly whisked
½ tablespoon Worcestershire sauce
Salt and powdered black pepper, as desired
Olive oil baking spray

Preparation:

1. In a mini food processor, put the onion, parsley, and garlic and process until finely cut up. 2. Transfer the onion mixture into a large-sized bowl. 3. Put in remaining ingredients except baking spray and blend to incorporate thoroughly. 4. Make equal-sized balls from the mixture. 5. Spray the inner basket of your Air Fryer with baking spray and slide it into the Air Fryer. 6. Set the Air Fryer at 200ºC to preheat for 4-5 minutes. 7. After preheating, place the meatballs in the preheated basket of Air Fryer. 8. Slide the basket inside and set the time for 12 minutes. 9. While cooking, turn the meatballs once halfway through. 10. After the cooking period is finished, take off the meatballs from Air Fryer and enjoy right away.

Nutritional Information per Serving: Calories: 243| Fat: 7.6g| Sat Fat: 3.2g| Carbohydrates: 7.8g| Fibre: 0.8g| Sugar: 1.9g| Protein: 33.2g

Stuffed Pork Roll

⏰ Prep Time: 15 minutes   🍲 Cook: 15 minutes   ⬥ Serves: 4

Ingredients:

1 scallion, cut up
35g sun-dried tomatoes, finely cut up
2 tablespoons fresh parsley, cut up
Salt and powdered black pepper, as desired
4 (170g) pork cutlets, pounded slightly
2 teaspoons paprika
½ tablespoons olive oil
Olive oil baking spray

Preparation:

1. In a bowl, blend together the scallion, tomatoes, parsley, salt, and black pepper. 2. Spread the tomato mixture over each pork cutlet. 3. Roll each cutlet and secure with cocktail sticks. 4. Rub the outer part of rolls with paprika, salt, and black pepper. 5. Coat the rolls with oil. 6. Spray the inner basket of your Air Fryer with baking spray and slide it into the Air Fryer. 7. Set the Air Fryer at 200ºC to preheat for 4-5 minutes. 8. After preheating, place the pork rolls in the preheated basket of Air Fryer. 9. Slide the basket inside and set the time for 15 minutes. 10. After the cooking period is finished, take off the pork rolls from Air Fryer and enjoy right away.

Nutritional Information per Serving: Calories: 244| Fat: 14.5g| Sat Fat: 2.7g| Carbohydrates: 19.3g| Fibre: 2.6g| Sugar: 1.7g| Protein: 14.2g

Beef Lasagna

⏰ **Prep Time:** 15 minutes   🍲 **Cook:** 40 minutes   🍂 **Serves:** 6

Ingredients:

455g Italian sausage
2 eggs
500g ricotta cheese
100g Parmesan cheese, grated
1 teaspoon garlic powder
½ teaspoon salt
½ teaspoon black pepper
Olive oil baking spray
680g marinara sauce
8 lasagna noodle sheets
10 basil leaves
454g mozzarella cheese, grated

Preparation:

1. Sizzle a wok on turner at around medium-high heat.2. Cook the sausage for around 8-10 minutes.3. Take off form burner and drain off any excess fat.4. Put the eggs, ricotta, Parmesan, garlic powder, salt, and pepper into a bowl and blend to incorporate.5. Spray a baking pan with baking spray.6. Spread a thin layer of marinara sauce in the bottom of baking pan. 7. Place the lasagna noodles over the marinara sauce.8. Place a layer of cheese mixture on top, followed by a layer of cooked sausage, basil leaves, mozzarella cheese and marinara sauce.9. Repeat the layers, ending with mozzarella cheese.10. With a piece of heavy-duty foil, cover the pan tightly. 11. Spray the inner basket of your Air Fryer with baking spray and then slide it in the Air Fryer.12. Set the Air Fryer at 170ºC to preheat for 4-5 minutes.13. After preheating, place the baking pan in the preheated basket of Air Fryer.14. Slide the basket back into the Air Fryer and set the time for 25 minutes.15. After 25 minutes of cooking, take off the foil from baking pan.16. Immediately set the Air Fryer at 140ºC to preheat for 5 minutes.17. After the cooking period is finished, take off the baking pan from Air Fryer and set it aside for around 5 minutes before enjoying.

Nutritional Information per Serving: Calories: 788| Fat: 52.4g| Sat Fat: 25.8g| Carbohydrates: 31.7g| Fibre: 3.1g| Sugar: 6g| Protein: 49.9g

Italian Sausages with Bell Peppers

⏰ **Prep Time:** 15 minutes   🍲 **Cook:** 15-18 minutes   🍂 **Serves:** 4

Ingredients:

4 Italian sausage links
3 small, multi-coloured bell peppers, seeded and sliced
½ of medium onion, sliced
1½ tablespoons olive oil
½ teaspoon dried basil
½ teaspoon garlic powder
Salt and ground black pepper, as desired
Olive oil baking spray

Preparation:

1. Put the bell peppers, onions, oil, basil, garlic powder, salt, and black pepper into a bowl and blend to incorporate.2. Spray the inner basket of your Air Fryer with baking spray and then slide it in the Air Fryer.3. Set the Air Fryer at 195ºC to preheat for 4-5 minutes.4. After preheating, place the bell pepper mixture in the preheated basket of Air Fryer. 5. Place the sausage links on top.6. Slide the basket back into the Air Fryer and set the time for 15-18 minutes.7. After the cooking period is finished, take off the bell pepper mixture and sausage links from Air Fryer and enjoy right away.

Nutritional Information per Serving: Calories: 768| Fat: 35.4g| Sat Fat: 8.8g| Carbohydrates: 45.7g| Fibre: 3.4g| Sugar: 6.5g| Protein: 63.9g

Spiced Pork Tenderloin

⏰ **Prep Time: 10 minutes**   🍲 **Cook: 22-25 minutes**   🍽 **Serves: 4**

Ingredients:

1 tablespoon brown sugar
1 tablespoon Italian seasoning
½ teaspoon cayenne powder
½ teaspoon paprika
½ teaspoon onion powder
½ teaspoon garlic powder
Salt and ground black pepper, as desired
570g pork tenderloin, silver skin removed
2 teaspoons olive oil
Olive oil baking spray

Preparation:

1. Put the brown sugar, Italian seasoning, spices, salt, and pepper into a small-sized bowl and blend to incorporate.2. Coat the pork tenderloin with oil and then rub with spice mixture.3. Spray the inner basket of your Air Fryer with baking spray and then slide it in the Air Fryer.4. Set the Air Fryer at 200ºC to preheat for 4-5 minutes.5. After preheating, place the pork tenderloin in the preheated basket of Air Fryer.6. Slide the basket back into the Air Fryer and set the time for 22-25 minutes.7. After the cooking period is finished, take off the pork tenderloin from Air Fryer and place onto a serving platter.8. Cut the pork tenderloin into serving portions and enjoy.

Nutritional Information per Serving: Calories: 288| Fat: 9.4g| Sat Fat: 2.8g| Carbohydrates: 5.7g| Fibre: 1.4g| Sugar: 2.5g| Protein: 43.9g

Crumb-Crusted Rack of Lamb

⏰ **Prep Time: 15 minutes**   🍲 **Cook: 30 minutes**   🍽 **Serves: 4**

Ingredients:

1 tablespoon butter, melted
1 garlic clove, finely cut up
800g rack of lamb
Salt and ground black pepper, as desired
1 egg
80g panko breadcrumbs
1 tablespoon fresh thyme, minced
1 tablespoon fresh rosemary, minced
Olive oil baking spray

Preparation:

1. In a bowl, blend together the butter, garlic, salt, and pepper.2. Coat the rack of lamb with garlic mixture.3. In a shallow dish, whisk the egg.4. In another dish, blend together the breadcrumbs and herbs.5. Dip the rack of lamb in the whisked egg and then, coat with the breadcrumbs mixture.6. Spray the inner basket of your Air Fryer with baking spray and then slide it in the Air Fryer.7. Set the Air Fryer at 100ºC to preheat for 4-5 minutes.8. After preheating, place the rack of lamb in the preheated basket of Air Fryer.9. Slide the basket back into the Air Fryer and set the time for 25 minutes.10. After 25 minutes of cooking, set the Air Fryer at 200ºC to cook for 5 minutes.11. After the cooking period is finished, take off the rack of lamb from Air Fryer and place onto a cutting board for around 5 minutes12. Cut the rack of lamb into individual chops and enjoy.

Nutritional Information per Serving: Calories: 288| Fat: 19.4g| Sat Fat: 6.8g| Carbohydrates: 6.7g| Fibre: 1.4g| Sugar: 0.5g| Protein: 33.9g

Flank Steak Pinwheels

⏰ **Prep Time: 15 minutes** 🍲 **Cook: 8-10 minutes** ❦ **Serves: 4**

Ingredients:

1 (455g) (½-inch thick) flank steak
1 tablespoon olive oil
2 teaspoons garlic, minced
2 teaspoons Italian seasoning
Salt and ground black pepper, as desired
285g frozen spinach, thawed
160g roasted red pepper, cut up
110g mozzarella cheese, shredded
Olive oil baking spray

Preparation:

1. Put the steak, oil, Italian seasoning, garlic, salt, and pepper into a bowl and blend to incorporate. 2. Put into your fridge to marinate for around 24 hours. 3. Place the steak onto a smooth surface. 4. Spread the spinach over steak, leaving a ¼-inch border. 5. Top with red pepper, followed by the cheese. 6. Tightly Roll up the steak. 7. Spray the inner basket of your Air Fryer with baking spray and then slide it in the Air Fryer. 8. Set the Air Fryer at 200°C to preheat for 4-5 minutes. 9. After preheating, place the steak roll in the preheated basket of Air Fryer. 10. Slide the basket back into the Air Fryer and set the time for 8-10 minutes. 11. After the cooking period is finished, take off the steak roll from Air Fryer and place onto a cutting board for around 10 minutes. 12. Cut the roll into serving portions and enjoy right away.

Nutritional Information per Serving: Calories: 313| Fat: 19g| Sat Fat: 6.8g| Carbohydrates: 5g| Fibre: 2g| Sugar: 1g| Protein: 33.9g

Chapter 6 Fish & Seafood Recipes

Crispy Tilapia Milanese

⏰ Prep Time: 10 minutes   🍲 Cook: 8-9 minutes   ❖ Serves: 2

Ingredients:

2 (115g) fillets tilapia fillets
30g all-purpose flour
1 egg
2 tablespoons lemon juice
¼ teaspoon salt
65g Italian-Seasoned bread crumbs
1 tablespoon lemon-pepper seasoning
Olive oil baking spray
1 lemon, cut into wedges

Preparation:

1. In a bowl, put the flour. 2. In a second bowl, whisk the eggs, salt, and lemon juice. 3. In a third bowl, put the breadcrumbs and lemon-pepper seasoning and blend to incorporate. 4. Coat the tilapia fillets with flour, then dip into egg mixture and finally coat with breadcrumb mixture. 5. Spray both sides of fish with baking spray. 6. Spray the inner basket of your Air Fryer with baking spray and slide it into the Air Fryer. 7. Set the Air Fryer at 200ºC to preheat for 4-5 minutes. 8. After preheating, place the tilapia fillets in the preheated basket of Air Fryer. 9. Slide the basket inside and set the time for 8-9 minutes. 10. After 5 minutes of cooking, turn the tilapia fillets. 11. After the cooking period is finished, take off the tilapia fillets from Air Fryer and enjoy right away with lemon wedges.

Nutritional Information per Serving: Calories: 324| Fat: 6.1g| Sat Fat: 2g| Carbohydrates: 34.3g| Fibre: 2.6g| Sugar: 3g| Protein: 32g

Rosemary Salmon

⏰ Prep Time: 10 minutes   🍲 Cook: 10 minutes   ❖ Serves: 2

Ingredients:

2 (170g) salmon fillets
2 tablespoons fresh rosemary, minced
Salt and powdered black pepper, as desired
1 tablespoon olive oil
Olive oil baking spray

Preparation:

1. Spray the inner basket of your Air Fryer with baking spray and slide it into the Air Fryer. 2. Set the Air Fryer at 180ºC to preheat for 4-5 minutes. 3. Sprinkle each salmon fillet with rosemary, salt, and black pepper, then coat with the oil. 4. After preheating, place the salmon fillets in the preheated basket of Air Fryer. 5. Slide the basket inside and set the time for 10 minutes. 6. While cooking, turn the salmon fillets once halfway through. 7. After the cooking period is finished, take off the salmon fillets from Air Fryer and enjoy right away.

Nutritional Information per Serving: Calories: 285| Fat: 17.6g| Sat Fat: 2.5g| Carbohydrates: 0.2g| Fibre: 0g| Sugar: 0g| Protein: 33.2g

Dill Cod with Green Beans

⏰ **Prep Time: 10 minutes** 🍲 **Cook: 12 minutes** 📚 **Serves: 2**

Ingredients:

Olive oil baking spray
For the Green Beans:
220g frozen green beans
1 tablespoon olive oil
Salt, as required
For the Cod:
1 garlic clove, minced
1 tablespoon fresh dill, chopped
1 tablespoon fresh lemon juice
1 tablespoon olive oil
Salt, as desired
2 (170g) cod fillets

Preparation:

1. Spray the inner basket of your Air Fryer with baking spray and slide it into the Air Fryer. 2. Set the Air Fryer at 190ºC to preheat for 4-5 minutes. 3. In a bowl, put the green beans, oil, and salt and toss to incorporate. 4. After preheating, place the green beans in the preheated basket of Air Fryer. 5. Slide the basket inside and set the time for 12 minutes. 6. Meanwhile, make the cod: in a bowl, put the cod and remaining ingredients and blend thoroughly. 7. After 6 minutes of cooking, flip the green beans. 8. Arrange the cod fillets on top of green beans. 9. After the cooking period is finished, take off the cod and green beans from Air Fryer and enjoy right away.

Nutritional Information per Serving: Calories: 334| Fat: 16.6g| Sat Fat: 2.9g| Carbohydrates: 11.3g| Fibre: 4.6g| Sugar: 2.1g| Protein: 35.2g

Lemony Herbed Cod

⏰ **Prep Time: 10 minutes** 🍲 **Cook: 8 minutes** 📚 **Serves: 4**

Ingredients:

1 tablespoon olive oil
2 teaspoons lemon juice
½ teaspoon dried rosemary
½ teaspoon dried thyme
½ teaspoon dried oregano
½ teaspoon paprika
½ teaspoon garlic powder
Salt and ground black pepper, as desired
4 (115g) cod fillets
Olive oil baking spray

Preparation:

1. Put the oil, lemon juice, herbs, spices, salt, and pepper into a bowl and blend to incorporate.2. Coat the cod fillets with oil mixture generously.3. Spray the inner basket of your Air Fryer with baking spray and then slide it in the Air Fryer.4. Set the Air Fryer at 200ºC to preheat for 4-5 minutes.5. After preheating, place the cod fillets in the preheated basket of Air Fryer.6. Slide the basket back into the Air Fryer and set the time for 8 minutes.7. After the cooking period is finished, take off the cod fillets from Air Fryer and enjoy right away.

Nutritional Information per Serving: Calories: 148| Fat: 6.4g| Sat Fat: 0.3g| Carbohydrates: 1g| Fibre: 0.1g| Sugar: 0g| Protein: 25g

Spiced Tilapia with Caper Sauce

⏰ **Prep Time: 10 minutes**   🍲 **Cook: 8 minutes**   ❖ **Serves: 2**

Ingredients:

Olive oil baking spray
For the Tilapia:
½ teaspoon garlic powder
½ teaspoon onion powder
½ teaspoon paprika
Salt and powdered black pepper, as desired
2 (115g) tilapia fillets
For the Caper Sauce:
1 tablespoon butter
1 tablespoon capers
1 tablespoon fresh lemon juice
Salt and black pepper, as desired
1 tbsp fresh parsley, finely cut up

Preparation:

1. Spray the inner basket of your Air Fryer with baking spray and slide it into the Air Fryer. 2. Set the Air Fryer at 200ºC to preheat for 4-5 minutes. 3. For the tilapia: put the spices, salt, and pepper into a bowl and blend thoroughly. 4. Rub both sides of the tilapia fillets with spice mixture. 5. After preheating, place the tilapia fillets in the preheated basket of Air Fryer. 6. Slide the basket inside and set the time for 8 minutes. 7. While cooking, turn the tilapia fillets once halfway through. 8. In the meantime, for the caper sauce: sizzle the butter into a small-sized wok on burner at medium-low heat. 9. Blend in remaining ingredients and take off from burner. 10. After the cooking period is finished, take off the tilapia fillets from Air Fryer and place onto serving plates. 11. Drizzle each fillet with caper sauce and enjoy right away.

Nutritional Information per Serving: Calories: 190| Fat: 8.1g| Sat Fat: 4g| Carbohydrates: 8.3g| Fibre: 3g| Sugar: 2g| Protein: 20.2g

Healthy Salmon with Asparagus

⏰ **Prep Time: 10 minutes**   🍲 **Cook: 11 minutes**   ❖ **Serves: 2**

Ingredients:

2 (170g) boneless salmon fillets
1½ tablespoons fresh lemon juice
1 tablespoon olive oil
2 tablespoons fresh parsley, roughly cut up
2 tablespoons fresh dill, roughly cut up
225g asparagus
Salt and powdered black pepper, as desired
Olive oil baking spray

Preparation:

1. Spray the inner basket of your Air Fryer with baking spray and slide it into the Air Fryer. 2. Set the Air Fryer at 200ºC to preheat for 4-5 minutes. 3. In a small-sized bowl, blend together the lemon juice, oil, herbs, salt, and black pepper. 4. In a large-sized bowl, mix together the salmon and ¾ of oil mixture. 5. In a second large-sized bowl, put the asparagus and remaining oil mixture and mix to incorporate. 6. After preheating, place the asparagus in the preheated basket of Air Fryer. 7. Slide the basket inside and set the time for 11 minutes. 8. After 3 minutes of cooking, place the salmon fillets on top of asparagus. 9. After the cooking period is finished, take off the salmon fillets and asparagus from Air Fryer and enjoy right away.

Nutritional Information per Serving: Calories: 322| Fat: 1.6g| Sat Fat: 2.9g| Carbohydrates: 7.3g| Fibre: 3.1g| Sugar: 2.3g| Protein: 36.2g

Clams Oreganata

⏰ **Prep Time: 15 minutes** 🍲 **Cook: 10 minutes** 🍽 **Serves: 4**

Ingredients:

750g canned clam meat, drained and minced
4 tablespoons butter
3 cloves garlic, minced
165g panko breadcrumbs
25g Parmesan cheese, grated
1 tablespoon parsley fresh, finely cut up
1 tablespoon fresh chives, finely cut up
1 teaspoon Worcestershire sauce
¼ teaspoon red pepper flakes
Salt and powdered black pepper, as desired
2 lemons, cut into wedges

Preparation:

1. In a large-sized pot, sizzle the butter on burner at medium heat. 2. Cook the garlic for around 30-60 seconds. 3. Take off the pot from burner and blend in the clam meat and remaining ingredients except for lemon wedges. 4. Stuff each clam shell with stuffing mixture. 5. Spray the inner basket of your Air Fryer with baking spray and slide it into the Air Fryer. 6. Set the Air Fryer at 200ºC to preheat for 4-5 minutes. 7. After preheating, place the stuffed clam shells in the preheated basket of Air Fryer. 8. Slide the basket inside and set the time for 6-8 minutes. 9. After the cooking period is finished, take off the stuffed clam shells from Air Fryer and enjoy with lemon wedges.

Nutritional Information per Serving: Calories: 154| Fat: 4g| Sat Fat: 2g| Carbohydrates: 10.3g| Fibre: 1g| Sugar: 2g| Protein: 20.2g

Crispy Parmesan Shrimp

⏰ **Prep Time: 15 minutes** 🍲 **Cook: 10 minutes** 🍽 **Serves: 3**

Ingredients:

50g Parmesan cheese, grated
2 cloves garlic, minced
2 tablespoons olive oil
½ teaspoon dried basil
½ teaspoon dried oregano
½ teaspoon onion powder
¼ teaspoon red pepper flakes, crushed
Powdered black pepper, as desired
455g shrimp, peeled and deveined
1 tablespoons fresh lemon juice
Olive oil baking spray

Preparation:

1. Spray the inner basket of your Air Fryer with baking spray and slide it into the Air Fryer. 2. Set the Air Fryer at 175ºC to preheat for 4-5 minutes. 3. In a large-sized bowl, put the Parmesan cheese, garlic, oil, herbs, and spices and blend to incorporate 4. Put in the shrimp and toss to coat well. 5. After preheating, place the shrimp in the preheated basket of Air Fryer. 6. Slide the basket inside and set the time for 10 minutes. 7. After the cooking period is finished, take off the shrimp from Air Fryer and enjoy right away.

Nutritional Information per Serving: Calories: 354| Fat: 13.6g| Sat Fat: 3.9g| Carbohydrates: 5.3g| Fibre: 0.3g| Sugar: 0.4g| Protein: 56.2g

Classic Shrimp Scampi

⏰ **Prep Time: 15 minutes**   🍲 **Cook: 7 minutes**   ❖ **Serves: 3**

Ingredients:

4 tablespoons salted butter
1 tablespoon fresh lemon juice
1 tablespoon garlic, minced
2 teaspoons red pepper flakes, crushed
455g shrimp, peeled and deveined
2 tablespoons fresh basil, cut up
1 tablespoon fresh chives, cut up
2 tablespoons chicken broth

Preparation:

1. Arrange a 7-inch round baking pan in the inner basket of your Air Fryer.2. Slide the basket inside and set at 160ºC to preheat for 4-5 minutes.3. After preheating, put the butter, lemon juice, garlic, and red pepper flakes in the heated pan and blend to incorporate.4. Slide the basket inside and set the time for 7 minutes. 5. After 2 minutes of cooking, blend in the shrimp, basil, chives, and broth.6. After the cooking period is finished, take off the baking pan from Air Fryer and enjoy right away.

Nutritional Information per Serving: Calories: 245| Fat: 15.7g| Sat Fat: 7.9g| Carbohydrates: 3.2g| Fibre: 0.3g| Sugar: 0.2g| Protein: 26.2g

Scallops in Butter Sauce

⏰ **Prep Time: 15 minutes**   🍲 **Cook: 6 minutes**   ❖ **Serves: 3**

Ingredients:

55g butter
2 cloves garlic, minced
½ tablespoon fresh rosemary, cut up
½ tablespoon fresh thyme, cut up
¼ teaspoon lemon zest, grated
455g sea scallops, side muscles removed
Salt and powdered black pepper, as desired

Preparation:

1. Sizzle the butter into a wok on burner at medium heat.2. Cook the garlic, herbs, and lemon zest for around 1 minute.3. Blend in the scallops, salt, and black pepper and cook for around 2 minutes.4. Take off from burnet and place the scallop mixture into a baking pan.5. Slide the inner basket of your Air Fryer into the Air Fryer and set at 175ºC to preheat for 4-5 minutes.6. After preheating, place the baking pan in the Air Fryer Basket.7. Slide the basket inside and set the time for 4 minutes. 8. After the cooking period is finished, take off the baking pan from Air Fryer and enjoy right away.

Nutritional Information per Serving: Calories: 275| Fat: 16.6g| Sat Fat: 8.9g| Carbohydrates: 4.8g| Fibre: 0.5g| Sugar: 0.1g| Protein: 26.2g

Dill Salmon Cakes

⏰ Prep Time: 15 minutes 🍲 Cook: 20 minutes ≋ Serves: 4

Ingredients:

140g pink salmon
1 tablespoon fresh dill, chopped
30g Panko breadcrumbs
2 sliced lemon wedges
1 tablespoon mayonnaise
Salt and black pepper, to taste
1 teaspoon Dijon mustard
Cooking spray, for greasing
1 medium-size egg

Preparation:

1. Clean the salmon by discarding the bones and skin and putting it in a mixing bowl.2. Whisk the egg, pepper, salt, mustard, salmon, dill, and mayonnaise together in a mixing bowl.3. Make small patties using your hands.4. Coat the patties with oil spray.5. Place the Panko breadcrumbs in a bowl and coat both sides of the patties in the Panko breadcrumbs.6. Preheat the Air Fryer at 200°C for 4-5 minutes7. After preheating, place the patties in the Air Fryer Basket and cook for around 6 minutes.8. Turn the patties halfway through the cooking time.9. After the cooking period is finished, remove from the Air Fryer and serve with lemon wedges.

Nutritional Information per Serving: Calories: 300| Fat: 14.8g| Sat Fat: 2.1g| Carbohydrates: 11g| Fibre: 1.5g| Sugar: 1.7g| Protein: 32.7g

Garlic Butter Lobster Tails with Olives

⏰ Prep Time: 5 minutes 🍲 Cook: 10 minutes ≋ Serves: 4

Ingredients:

2 garlic cloves, minced
2 tablespoons butter, melted
1 teaspoon onion powder
910g fresh lobster tails, cleaned and halved, in shells
1 teaspoon cayenne pepper
Salt and ground black pepper, to taste
150g green olives

Preparation:

1. Set the Air Fryer at 185°C to preheat for 4-5 minutes.2. Thoroughly combine all ingredients in a ziploc bag and shake to combine well.3. After preheating, grease the Air Fryer basket with cooking oil spray.4. Transfer the coated lobster tails to the Air Fryer basket.5. Cook for 9 to 10 minutes, shaking the basket midway through the cooking. Cook in batches.6. Once finished, serve with green olives and enjoy!

Nutritional Information per Serving: Calories: 232| Fat: 19g| Sat Fat: 11g| Carbohydrates: 4g| Fibre: 1g| Sugar: 0.1g| Protein: 15g

Roasted Tuna with Linguine

Prep Time: 15 minutes | Cook: 20 minutes | Serves: 2

Ingredients:

340g linguine, cooked according to package directions
455g fresh tuna fillets
1 tablespoon olive oil
120g parsley leaves, chopped
Salt and black pepper, to taste
1 tablespoon capers, chopped
Juice from 1 lemon

Preparation:

1. Preheat the Air Fryer at 175ºC for 4-5 minutes. 2. Season the tuna with salt and pepper. Brush with olive oil. 3. After preheating, place the tuna in the Air Fryer Basket. 4. Slide the basket inside and set the time for 20 minutes. 5. Once the tuna is cooked, shred it with forks and place it on top of the cooked linguine. Add the capers and parsley. 6. Season with the salt and pepper and add the lemon juice. 7. Serve and enjoy.

Nutritional Information per Serving: Calories: 520| Fat: 9.6g| Sat Fat: 3g| Carbohydrates: 60g| Fibre: 3g| Sugar: 1g| Protein: 35g

Roasted Tuna with Capers

Prep Time: 5 minutes | Cook: 15 minutes | Serves: 4

Ingredients:

910g boneless tuna fillets
1 tablespoon coriander, chopped
2 tablespoons mustard
1 tablespoon olive oil
Juice of 1 lime
2 tablespoons capers, drained
1 teaspoon mustard seeds, crushed
A pinch of salt and black pepper

Preparation:

1. Set the Air Fryer at 195ºC to preheat for 4-5 minutes. 2. Mix the tuna with mustard and the rest of the ingredients in a baking pan and toss well. 3. After preheating, transfer the baking pan to the Air Fryer basket. 4. Cook for around 15 minutes. 5. Once finished, divide between plates and serve.

Nutritional Information per Serving: Calories: 240| Fat: 13g| Sat Fat: 1.7g| Carbohydrates: 6g| Fibre: 0.7g| Sugar: 1g| Protein: 15g

Simple Cod with Pesto

Prep Time: 10 minutes | Cook: 20 minutes | Serves: 4

Ingredients:

4 (170g) cod fillets
2 teaspoons olive oil
Pinch of salt
Olive oil baking spray
60g pesto

Preparation:

1. Spray the inner basket of your Air Fryer with baking spray and slide it into the Air Fryer. 2. Set the Air Fryer at 130ºC to preheat for 4-5 minutes. 3. Drizzle the cod fillets with oil and sprinkle with a pinch of salt. 4. After preheating, place the cod fillets in the preheated basket of Air Fryer. 5. Slide the basket inside and set the time for 20 minutes. 6. After the cooking period is finished, take off the cod fillets from Air Fryer and place onto a platter. 7. Top with the pesto and enjoy right away.

Nutritional Information per Serving: Calories: 380| Fat: 24.6g| Sat Fat: 3.9g| Carbohydrates: g| Fibre: 0.6g| Sugar: 2g| Protein: 36.2g

Chapter 6 Fish & Seafood Recipes

Tasty Shrimp Risotto

⏱ **Prep Time: 5 minutes** 🍲 **Cook: 32 minutes** ❖ **Serves: 2**

Ingredients:

2 tablespoons olive oil
1 small onion, finely cut up
2 cloves garlic, minced
2 tablespoons butter
270g risotto rice, rinsed
720ml hot chicken broth
170g shrimp, peeled and deveined
2-3 tablespoons Parmesan cheese, shredded
1 tablespoon fresh parsley, cut up

Preparation:

1. Arrange a round baking pan in the inner basket of your Air Fryer. 2. Slide the basket back into the Air Fryer and set the Air Fryer at 200ºC to preheat for 4-5 minutes. 3. After preheating, carefully place the oil in the heated baking pan. 4. Swirl the pan to coat with oil evenly. 5. In the pan, put the onion and garlic and with a wooden spoon, blend with oil. 6. Slide the basket back into the Air Fryer and set the time for 12 minutes. 7. After 4 minutes of cooking, put the butter into the pan. 8. After 6 minutes of cooking, put the and rice into the pan and blend. 9. After 7 minutes of cooking, put in 240ml of broth and blend. 10. After 12 minutes of cooking, put in remaining broth and blend. 11. Immediately set the Air Fryer at 175ºC to cook for 20 minutes. 12. After 10 minutes of cooking, put the shrimp into the pan and blend thoroughly. 13. After the cooking period is finished, take off the baking pan from Air Fryer and immediately blend in cheese and parsley. 14. Set it aside for around 5 minutes before enjoying.

Nutritional Information per Serving: Calories: 535| Fat: 20.4g| Sat Fat: 8g| Carbohydrates: 45.7g| Fibre: g| Sugar: 6.5g| Protein: 26.9g

Lemon Roasted Whole Branzino

⏱ **Prep Time: 10 minutes** 🍲 **Cook: 13-15 minutes** ❖ **Serves: 2**

Ingredients:

2 whole branzino fish, cleaned
½ lemon, cut into slices
4 cloves garlic, sliced
1 teaspoon dried thyme
Salt and ground black pepper, as desired
Olive oil baking spray

Preparation:

1. Insert the lemon and garlic slices in the cavity of each fish. 2. Sprinkle the cavity of each fish with half of thyme, salt, and pepper. 3. Sprinkle the outer side of each fish with remaining thyme, salt, and pepper. 4. Spray the inner basket of your Air Fryer with baking spray and then slide it in the Air Fryer. 5. Set the Air Fryer at 200ºC to preheat for 4-5 minutes. 6. After preheating, place both fish in the preheated basket of Air Fryer. 7. Slide the basket back into the Air Fryer and set the time for 13-15 minutes. 8. After the cooking period is finished, take off the fish from Air Fryer and enjoy right away.

Nutritional Information per Serving: Calories: 255| Fat: 5g| Sat Fat: 2g| Carbohydrates: 1.5g| Fibre: 0.1g| Sugar: 0.1g| Protein: 47.9g

Spicy Roasted Salmon

⏱ **Prep Time: 10 minutes** 🍲 **Cook: 10 minutes** ◈ **Serves: 4**

Ingredients:

4 (115g) salmon fillets
2 tablespoons brown sugar
1 teaspoon Italian seasoning
1 teaspoon red chilli powder
½ teaspoon paprika
1 teaspoon garlic powder
Salt and ground black pepper, as desired
Olive oil baking spray

Preparation:

1. Put the brown sugar, Italian seasoning, spices, salt, and pepper into a small-sized bowl and blend to incorporate. 2. Rub the salmon fillets with seasoning mixture generously. 3. Spray the inner basket of your Air Fryer with baking spray and then slide it in the Air Fryer. 4. Set the Air Fryer at 200ºC to preheat for 4-5 minutes. 5. After preheating, place the salmon fillets in the preheated basket of Air Fryer. 6. Slide the basket back into the Air Fryer and set the time for 10 minutes. 7. While cooking, flip the salmon fillets once halfway through. 8. After the cooking period is finished, take off the salmon fillets from Air Fryer and enjoy right away.

Nutritional Information per Serving: Calories: 192| Fat: 7.4g| Sat Fat: 1g| Carbohydrates: 6.7g| Fibre: 1g| Sugar: 6g| Protein: 23.9g

Parmesan Crusted Tilapia

⏱ **Prep Time: 10 minutes** 🍲 **Cook: 8-10 minutes** ◈ **Serves: 4**

Ingredients:

60g all-purpose flour
1 teaspoon garlic powder
¼ teaspoon cayenne pepper
Salt, as desired
2 large eggs
120g panko breadcrumbs
55g Parmesan cheese, grated
4 (115g) tilapia fillets
Olive oil baking spray

Preparation:

1. Put the flour, garlic powder, cayenne pepper, and salt into a shallow dish and blend. 2. Whisk the eggs into a second shallow dish. 3. Pu the breadcrumbs and Parmesan cheese in a third shallow dish and blend. 4. Sprinkle the tilapia fillets with salt. 5. Coat the tilapia fillets with flour mixture, then dip into eggs and finally coat with panko mixture. 6. Spray the top of fillets with baking spray. 7. Spray the inner basket of your Air Fryer with baking spray and then slide it in the Air Fryer. 8. Set the Air Fryer at 200ºC to preheat for 4-5 minutes. 9. After preheating, place the tilapia fillets in the preheated basket of Air Fryer. 10. Slide the basket back into the Air Fryer and set the time for 8-10 minutes. 11. After the cooking period is finished, take off the tilapia fillets from Air Fryer and enjoy right away.

Nutritional Information per Serving: Calories: 580| Fat: 33.4g| Sat Fat: 5.8g| Carbohydrates: 27.7g| Fibre: 1g| Sugar: 0.5g| Protein: 38.9g

Chapter 7 Dessert Recipes

Cheesecake Bites

⏰ Prep Time: 15 minutes 🍲 Cook: 2 minutes ❖ Serves: 12

Ingredients:

230g cream cheese, softened
100g plus 2 tablespoons sugar, divided
4 tablespoons heavy cream, divided
½ teaspoon vanilla extract
120g almond flour
Olive oil baking spray

Preparation:

1. In a bowl of a stand blender, fitted with paddle attachment, put the cream cheese, 100g of sugar, 2 tablespoons of heavy cream, and vanilla extract and whisk to form a smooth mixture. 2. With a scooper, scoop the mixture onto a bakery paper-lined baking tray. Freeze for around 30 minutes. 3. In a small-sized bowl, put the remaining cream. 4. In another small-sized bowl, put the almond flour and remaining sugar and blend to incorporate. 5. Dip each cheesecake bite in cream and then coat with the flour mixture. 6. Spray the inner basket of your Air Fryer with baking spray and slide it into the Air Fryer. 7. Set the Air Fryer at 150ºC to preheat for 4-5 minutes. 8. After preheating, place the cheesecake bites in the preheated basket of Air Fryer. 9. Slide the basket inside and set the time for 2 minutes. 10. After the cooking period is finished, take off the cheesecake bites from Air Fryer and transfer tonto a platter. 11. Enjoy moderately hot.

Nutritional Information per Serving: Calories: 128| Fat: 9g| Sat Fat: 5.3g| Carbohydrates: 10.9g| Fibre: 0.1g| Sugar: 10.1g| Protein: 1.8g

Sweet Dough Balls

⏰ Prep Time: 15 minutes 🍲 Cook: 6 minutes ❖ Serves: 8

Ingredients:

455g pizza dough, prepared
85g powdered sugar
2-3 tablespoons milk
Olive oil baking spray

Preparation:

1. Spray the inner basket of your Air Fryer with baking spray and slide it into the Air Fryer. 2. Set the Air Fryer at 170ºC to preheat for 4-5 minutes. 3. Shape the dough into small-sized balls. 4. After preheating, place the dough balls in the preheated basket of Air Fryer. 5. Slide the basket inside and set the time for 6 minutes. 6. While cooking, turn the dough balls once halfway through. 7. In the meantime, in a small-sized bowl, put the powdered sugar and milk and blend to incorporate. 8. After the cooking period is finished, take off the dough balls from Air Fryer and place onto a platter. 9. Dip the dough balls into the milk mixture. 10. Set aside to cool slightly before enjoying.

Nutritional Information per Serving: Calories: 171| Fat: 2g| Sat Fat: 1g| Carbohydrates: 35g| Fibre: 1g| Sugar: 11g| Protein: 4g g

Easy Vanilla Biscotti

⏰ **Prep Time: 15 minutes**   🍳 **Cook: 12 minutes**   🍽 **Serves: 8**

Ingredients:

120g all-purpose flour
3 tablespoons olive oil
65g sugar
2 eggs
1 teaspoon baking powder
1 teaspoon vanilla extract
Olive oil baking spray

Preparation:

1. Spray the inner basket of your Air Fryer with baking spray and slide it into the Air Fryer.2. Set the Air Fryer at 160ºC to preheat for 4-5 minutes.3. Put the flour and remaining ingredients except baking spray into a bowl and blend to incorporate. Shape the dough into a log.4. After preheating, place the log in the preheated basket of Air Fryer.5. Slide the basket inside and set the time for 7 minutes.6. After the cooking period is finished, take off the log from Air Fryer and place onto a cooling metal rack for 10 minutes.7. Cut the loaf into 1-inch pieces.8. Again, spray the inner basket of your Air Fryer with baking spray and slide it into the Air Fryer.9. Set the Air Fryer at 160ºC to preheat for 4-5 minutes.10. After preheating, place the biscotti in the preheated basket of Air Fryer.11. Slide the basket inside and set the time for 5 minutes.12. After the cooking period is finished, take off the biscotti from Air Frye r and place onto a cooling metal rack for 5 minutes before enjoying.

Nutritional Information per Serving: Calories: 152| Fat: 3g| Sat Fat: 1g| Carbohydrates: 20.3g| Fibre: 0.6g| Sugar: 8g| Protein: 3g

Banana Yoghurt Cake

⏰ **Prep Time: 15 minutes**   🍳 **Cook: 35 minutes**   🍽 **Serves: 5**

Ingredients:

Olive oil baking spray
60g all-purpose flour
30g whole-wheat flour
¼ teaspoon baking soda
½ teaspoon salt
1 large-sized egg
100g granulated sugar
60g plain Greek yoghurt
60ml olive oil
½ teaspoon pure vanilla extract
2 ripe bananas, peeled and mashed
2 tablespoons turbinado sugar

Preparation:

1. Spray a cake pan with baking spray.2. In a bowl, sift together the flours, baking soda, and salt.3. In another large-sized bowl, put the egg, granulated sugar, yoghurt, oil, and vanilla extract and whisk to incorporate.4. Put in the bananas and whisk to incorporate thoroughly.5. Now, put the flour mixture and blend until just incorporated.6. Place the mixture into the cake pan and sprinkle with the turbinado sugar.7. Slide the inner basket of your Air Fryer into the Air Fryer and set at 155ºC to preheat for 4-5 minutes.8. After preheating, place the cake pan in the Air Fryer Basket.9. Slide the basket inside and set the time for 35 minutes. 10. After the cooking period is finished, take off the cake pan from Air Fryer and place onto a cooling metal rack for around 10-15 minutes.11. Carefully invert the cake onto the metal rack to cool thoroughly.12. Cut the bread into slices and enjoy.

Nutritional Information per Serving: Calories: 313| Fat: 11.7g| Sat Fat: 1.9g| Carbohydrates: 50g| Fibre: 2.4g| Sugar: 30.3g| Protein: 4.8g

| Chapter 7 Dessert Recipes

Semolina Cake

⏱ **Prep Time: 15 minutes** 🍲 **Cook: 15-20 minutes** ❖ **Serves: 5**

Ingredients:

420g semolina
120ml olive oil
240ml milk
245g plain Greek yoghurt
200g sugar
½ teaspoon baking soda
1½ teaspoons baking powder
A pinch of salt
35g raisins
30g walnuts, cut up

Preparation:

1. In a bowl, put the semolina, oil, milk, yoghurt, and sugar and blend to incorporate.2. Cover and set aside for around 15 minutes.3. Put in the baking soda, baking powder, and salt in the bowl of semolina mixture and blend to incorporate thoroughly.4. Fold in the raisins and walnuts.5. Put the mixture into a cake pan.6. Slide the inner basket of your Air Fryer into the Air Fryer and set at 200ºC to preheat for 4-5 minutes.7. After preheating, place the cake pan in the Air Fryer Basket.8. Slide the basket inside and set the time for 15-20 minutes. 9. After the cooking period is finished, take off the cake pan from Air Fryer and place onto a cooling metal rack to cool for around 10 minutes.10. Now, invert the cake onto the metal rack to cool thoroughly before slicing.11. Cut the cake into serving portions and enjoy.

Nutritional Information per Serving: Calories: 634| Fat: 22.6g| Sat Fat: 8.9g| Carbohydrates: 91.3g| Fibre: 1.6g| Sugar: 40.3g| Protein: 13.2g

Perfect Chocolate Cheesecake

⏱ **Prep Time: 15 minutes** 🍲 **Cook: 30 minutes** ❖ **Serves: 6**

Ingredients:

Olive oil baking spray
3 eggs, whites and yolks separated
160g white chocolate, cut up
115g cream cheese, softened
2 tablespoons cocoa powder

Preparation:

1. Spray a cake pan with baking spray.2. In a bowl, put the egg whites and put into your fridge to chill before using.3. In a microwave-safe bowl, put the chocolate and microwave on high heat for around 2 minutes, stirring after every 30 seconds.4. In the bowl of chocolate, put the cream cheese and microwave for around 1-2 minutes or until cream cheese melts thoroughly.5. Take off from the microwave and blend in cocoa powder and egg yolks.6. Take off the egg whites from refrigerator and whisk until firm peaks form.7. Add ⅓ of the whipped egg whites into cheese mixture and gently blend to incorporate. Fold in the remaining egg whites.8. Place the mixture into the cake pan.9. Slide the inner basket of your Air Fryer into the Air Fryer and set at 140ºC to preheat for 4-5 minutes.10. After preheating, place the cake pan in the Air Fryer Basket.11. Slide the basket inside and set the time for 30 minutes. 12. After the cooking period is finished, take off the cake pan from Air Fryer and set aside to cool thoroughly.13. Put into your fridge to chill before enjoying.

Nutritional Information per Serving: Calories: 278| Fat: 16.6g| Sat Fat: 7.9g| Carbohydrates: 28.3g| Fibre: 0.6g| Sugar: 23.3g| Protein: 50.2g

Lemon Ricotta Cheesecake

⏰ **Prep Time: 10 minutes**   🍲 **Cook: 25 minutes**   🍃 **Serves: 8**

Ingredients:

505g ricotta cheese
3 eggs
150g sugar
3 tablespoons corn starch
1 tablespoon fresh lemon juice
2 teaspoons vanilla extract
1 teaspoon fresh lemon zest, finely grated

Preparation:

1. Slide the inner basket of your Air Fryer into the Air Fryer and set at 160ºC to preheat for 4-5 minutes.2. In a large-sized bowl, put all ingredients and blend to incorporate thoroughly.3. Place the mixture into a baking pan.4. After preheating, place the baking pan in the Air Fryer Basket.5. Slide the basket inside and set the time for 25 minutes. 6. After the cooking period is finished, take off the baking pan from Air Fryer and set aside for around 1-2 hours to cool.7. Put into your fridge to chill for around 2-3 hours before enjoying.

Nutritional Information per Serving: Calories: 197| Fat: 6.6g| Sat Fat: 1.9g| Carbohydrates: 25.3g| Fibre: 9.6g| Sugar: 1.3g| Protein: 20.2g

Sweet Apple Pie

⏰ **Prep Time: 15 minutes**   🍲 **Cook: 25 minutes**   🍃 **Serves: 3**

Ingredients:

70g butter, cut up and divided
100g flour
1 egg yolk
30g sugar
1 large-sized granny smith apple, peeled, cored and cut into 12 wedges

Preparation:

1. In a bowl, put half of the butter, flour, and egg yolk and blend until a soft dough forms.2. Put the dough onto a floured surface and roll into a 6-inch round circle.3. In a baking pan, put the remaining butter and sprinkle with sugar.4. Top with the apple wedges in a circular pattern.5. Place the rolled dough over apple wedges and gently press along the edges of the pan.6. Slide the inner basket of your Air Fryer into the Air Fryer and set at 200ºC to preheat for 4-5 minutes.7. After preheating, place the baking pan in the Air Fryer Basket.8. Slide the basket inside and set the time for 25 minutes. 9. After the cooking period is finished, take off the baking pan from Air Fryer and enjoy moderately hot.

Nutritional Information per Serving: Calories: 381| Fat: 21g| Sat Fat: 8.9g| Carbohydrates: 44.3g| Fibre: 16.6g| Sugar: 16.3g| Protein: 4.2g

Chocolate Croissants

⏱ **Prep Time: 10 minutes**   🍳 **Cook: 15 minutes**   ❖ **Serves: 3-4**

Ingredients:

35g chocolate chips
1 package Pillsbury crescent rolls
2 tablespoons melted butter
3 tablespoons Nutella
2 teaspoon sugar
Powdered sugar

Preparation:

1. Set the Air Fryer at 175ºC to preheat for 4-5 minutes. 2. Unroll the crescent rolls and divide them into triangles. 3. Spread 1 teaspoon Nutella on the wide end of each triangle, then curl the dough toward the tip to form a crescent shape. Tuck the sides slightly to seal in the filling. 4. In a small bowl, combine the melted butter with sugar. Brush the mixture on both sides of each crescent roll. 5. After preheating, place the crescent rolls in the Air Fryer basket, allowing a small space between them. 6. Air fry for 8 to 10 minutes or until golden brown and cooked through. 7. Melt the chocolate chips in the microwave at 15-second intervals, stirring between each one until smooth. Stir in the remaining Nutella. 8. Once the croissants are finished, dust them with the powdered sugar and drizzle with the chocolate sauce. Serve warm and enjoy!

Nutritional Information per Serving: Calories: 297| Fat: 16g| Sat Fat: 8.8g| Carbohydrates: 33g| Fibre: 1.9g| Sugar: 12g| Protein: 5.7g

Peach Cobbler

⏱ **Prep Time: 10 minutes**   🍳 **Cook: 15 minutes**   ❖ **Serves: 3-4**

Ingredients:

595g peach pie filling
200g of sugar
30g of flour
Cobbler Topping:
50g sugar
1 teaspoon baking powder
120g flour
1 teaspoon ground cinnamon
60ml milk
1 egg

Preparation:

1. Set the Air Fryer at 175ºC to preheat for 4-5 minutes. 2. Start by mixing the peach pie filling, sugar, and flour together. Make sure that all of the peaches are well-coated. 3. Lightly coat an Air Fryer-safe baking pan with olive oil or nonstick spray. 4. Spread the peach filling evenly in the bottom of the pan. 5. In another bowl, add 120g flour, 50g sugar, milk, baking powder, powdered cinnamon, and egg until well blended. 6. Spread the cobbler topping evenly over the peach filling in the pan, leaving some gaps to allow the peaches to peek through. 7. After preheating, place the pan in the Air Fryer Basket. Cook for approximately 10-15 minutes or until the topping is golden brown and fully cooked. 8. Remove the cobbler from the Air Fryer. 9. Set aside to cool before serving it.

Nutritional Information per Serving: Calories: 330| Fat: 11g| Sat Fat: 5g| Carbohydrates: 46g| Fibre: 1g| Sugar: 28g| Protein: 11.2g

Delicious Cannoli

⏱ **Prep Time: 25 minutes** 🍳 **Cook: 6 minutes** ⬧ **Serves: 12**

Ingredients:

For the Dough:
240g all-purpose flour
2 teaspoons granulated sugar
1 pinch sea salt
2 tablespoons cold butter, cut into small-sized cubes
1 large-sized egg yolk
120ml dry white wine

For the Filling:
250g ricotta cheese
125g powdered sugar
½ teaspoon powdered cinnamon
235g heavy whipping cream

For the Decoration:
60g mini chocolate chips
Powdered sugar, as desired

Preparation:

1. In a medium-sized bowl, blend together the flour, sugar, and salt. 2. With a pastry cutter, cut into cold butter to forms coarse crumbs. 3. Put in the egg yolk and wine and blend to form a crumbly dough. 4. Place the dough onto a lightly floured surface and with your hands, knead into a dough ball. 5. With plastic wrap, cover the dough and place in your fridge. 6. For the filling: in a large-sized bowl, blend together the ricotta, powdered sugar, and cinnamon. 7. Place the whipping cream in a large-sized bowl and with a hand blender, whisk to form stiff peaks. 8. Gently fold the whipped cream into the ricotta mixture. 9. Place the bowl of filling in your fridge before using. 10. Place the dough onto a floured surface and divide into 4 portions. 11. Roll each dough portion into ⅛-inch thickness. 12. With a cookie cutter, cut into 4-inch circles. 13. Spray the cannoli forms with baking spray. 14. Wrap each dough circle around the form. 15. With wet fingers, press down gently to seal. 16. Spray the outsides of the dough with baking spray. 17. Spray the inner basket of your Air Fryer with baking spray and slide it into the Air Fryer. 18. Set the Air Fryer at 200ºC to preheat for 4-5 minutes. 19. After preheating, place half of cannoli forms in the preheated basket of Air Fryer. 20. Slide the basket inside and set the time for 4-6 minutes. 21. After the cooking period is finished, take off the cannoli forms from Air Fryer. 22. Carefully remove the shells from cannoli forms. 23. Repeat with the remaining shells. Set the shells aside to cool thoroughly. 24. Place the filling mixture into a piping bag. Pipe the filling into the shells. 25. Dip the ends in the chocolate chips. Dust with powdered sugar and enjoy.

Nutritional Information per Serving: Calories: 210| Fat: 11g| Sat Fat: 6g| Carbohydrates: 23g| Fibre: 1g| Sugar: 10g| Protein: 4g

Honey Cake with Almonds and Pistachios

⏱ **Prep Time: 10 minutes** 🍳 **Cook: 25 minutes** ⬧ **Serves: 2**

Ingredients:

450g butter
100g chopped almonds
240g flour
1 tablespoon brown sugar
3 egg whites
680g honey
1 tablespoon baking powder
2 tablespoons sugar
120g chopped pistachios

Preparation:

1. Set the Air Fryer at 150ºC to preheat for 4-5 minutes. 2. In a bowl, add the butter and flour. 3. Mix the sugar, egg whites, brown sugar, and baking powder. 4. Pour the mixture into the round baking pan. 5. After preheating, place the baking pan in the Air Fryer Basket. 6. Cook for around 15 minutes in the Air Fryer. 7. Once ready, cover the cake with honey and garnish with pistachios. 8. Add the almonds on top to serve and enjoy!

Nutritional Information per Serving: Calories: 330| Fat: 12g| Sat Fat: 1.1g| Carbohydrates: 53g| Fibre: 1g| Sugar: 35g| Protein: 3.3g

Strawberry Cheesecake

⏰ **Prep Time: 20 minutes** 🍳 **Cook: 1 hour 37 minutes**
🍰 **Serves: 10**

Ingredients:

Olive oil baking spray
For the Crust:
7 tablespoons almond flour
2 tablespoons natural peanut butter
1 tablespoon honey
For the Filling:
2 eggs
300g plain Greek yoghurt
300g cream cheese
2 scoops vanilla whey protein powder
2 tablespoons strawberry preserves
2 tablespoons Splenda
¼ teaspoon vanilla extract
145g fresh strawberries, hulled and sliced
For the Topping:
2 tablespoons fat-free plain Greek yoghurt
1 tablespoon Splenda
2 tablespoons vanilla whey protein powder

Preparation:

1. Slide the inner basket of your Air Fryer into the Air Fryer and set at 120ºC to preheat for 4-5 minutes. 2. Line a round baking pan with bakery paper and them lightly spray it with baking spray. 3. For the crust: add ingredients in a bowl and blend to form a dough ball. 4. Place the dough ball in the centre of baking pan. 5. With your fingers, press downwards until the dough spreads in the bottom of pan. 6. After preheating, place the baking pan in the Air Fryer Basket. 7. Slide the basket inside and set the time for 7 minutes. 8. After the cooking period is finished, take off the baking pan from Air Fryer and set aside to cool slightly. 9. In the meantime, for the filling: in a large-sized bowl, put the eggs and remaining ingredients except strawberries and whisk to form a smooth mixture. Fold in the strawberries. 10. Place strawberry mixture over the crust. With the back of spatula, smooth the top surface of strawberry mixture. 11. Again, set your Air Fryer at 120ºC. 12. Arrange baking pan in the Air Fryer Basket. 13. Slide the basket inside and set the time for 30 minutes. 14. After 30 minutes of cooking, set your Air Fryer at 90ºC for 1 hour. 15. After the cooking period is finished, take off the baking pan from Air Fryer and set aside for around 1-2 hours to cool. 16. For the topping: add ingredients in a bowl and blend to incorporate. 17. After cooling, top the cheesecake with topping mixture. 18. Put into your fridge for around 4-8 hours before enjoying.

Nutritional Information per Serving: Calories: 394| Fat: 25.6g| Sat Fat: 11.9g| Carbohydrates: 18.3g| Fibre: 5.6g| Sugar: 14.3g| Protein: 20.2g

Chocolate Cream Puffs

⏰ **Prep Time: 15 minutes** 🍳 **Cook: 35 minutes** 🍰 **Serves: 4**

Ingredients:

2 tablespoons brown sugar
120ml almond milk
2 tablespoons almond butter
2 eggs
60g all-purpose flour
240g chocolate sauce

Preparation:

1. Set the Air Fryer at 175ºC to preheat for 4-5 minutes. 2. Add the butter, almond milk, and sugar to the saucepan. Bring the mixture to a boil. 3. Remove the saucepan from the heat. Then, put the flour in the milk and stir it well until a thick dough forms. Allow the mixture to cool slightly. 4. Add the eggs to the mixture and create the dough from the mixture. 5. After preheating, line the Air Fryer basket with parchment paper. 6. Pipe this dough into rounds with a piping bag in the Air Fryer Basket. 7. Air fry for around 35 minutes or until they are golden and puffed. 8. After the cooking period is finished, take off the puffs from the Air Fryer. 9. Once the puffs are cooled enough, create a hole in the bottom of the puff to fill with chocolate sauce using a piping bag. You can fill with cream if desired. 10. Top the puff with additional chocolate sauce if desired. 11. Serve and enjoy.

Nutritional Information per Serving: Calories: 220| Fat: 9g| Sat Fat: 7g| Carbohydrates: 26g| Fibre: 1g| Sugar: 17g| Protein: 3g

Conclusion

The Colourful Italian Food Air Fryer Cookbook for the UK is more than just a collection of recipes—it's your key to mastering Italian cuisine with modern convenience. By blending traditional flavours with the innovative capabilities of the air fryer, this cookbook empowers you to create memorable meals with minimal effort and maximum satisfaction.

From comforting pasta bakes to golden, flaky pastries, each recipe has been thoughtfully crafted to bring the essence of Italy into your home. Whether you're serving hearty lasagne for a family gathering or whipping up a quick bruschetta for yourself, you'll find joy in every dish. The air fryer not only saves time and reduces oil but also delivers the perfect texture and taste that Italian food is known for.

As you explore these pages, you'll discover how versatile your air fryer can be, from roasting vegetables to baking desserts, all with a uniquely Italian twist. The detailed instructions and helpful tips ensure that even novice cooks can achieve outstanding results.

Thank you for choosing this cookbook as your guide to Italian air fryer cooking. May it inspire countless delicious meals, shared with loved ones around the table. With every crispy bite and flavourful dish, you'll deepen your love for Italian cuisine—effortlessly and deliciously. Buon appetito, and happy cooking!

Printed in Great Britain
by Amazon